Murder In The Streets

A White Choctaw Witness To The 1921 Tulsa Race Massacre

By William C. "Choc" Phillips

EAKIN PRESS ⚜ Fort Worth, Texas
www.EakinPress.com

Contents

PROLOGUE: Hannibal B. Johnson

God gave Noah the rainbow sign
No more water, the fire next time

Hatred, which could destroy so much, never failed to destroy the man who hated,
and this was an immutable law.

James Baldwin, *The Fire Next Time* (1963)

Eyewitness. White witness. Cooperating witness.

Seer. Sayer. Storyteller.

William C. "Choc" Phillips, born December 1, 1901, in Greer County in southwest Oklahoma as the oldest of eight children, arrived in Tulsa in 1918. Although a Choctaw Indian by birth, one-eighth "by blood," he lived his life as a white man in a white world.

At the time of the 1921 Tulsa Race Massacre, Phillips worked as an usher in the Royal Theatre at 402 South Main Street, an 800-seat venue managed by Arthur G. Ellis. An untrained but talented baritone, he and a few friends were harmonizing even as the disaster unfolded. Phillips later sang in and managed vaudeville shows.

In 1938, Phillips joined the Tulsa Police Department where, as a founding member of the Barbershop Quartet Singing Society, he toured the country touting Tulsa. Conscripted into the military, he did two years in the United States Coast Guard (1942 – 1944) as a shore patrolman stationed in St. Louis during World War II, and then returned to his civilian policing post.

Phillips served the City of Tulsa as a police officer for twenty-six years, at one point helming the Fraternal Order of Police. He blazed trails during his decades-long stint with the Tulsa Police Department. He formed the inaugural school crossing guard program for Tulsa Public Schools. He launched a police department retirement program that became a national model.

1

Phillips retired from the Tulsa Police Department in 1966. He transitioned to the life of a cattle rancher, relocating to Leonard, Okla.. There, his life ended on December 10, 1991.

Phillips, this white Choctaw, bore witness to an act of anti-Blackness that defined a period commonly known as the "nadir of race relations in America." He compiled a manuscript later in his life, but it remained unpublished.

Phillips lived to tell his fly-on-the-wall tale, but, until now, post-mortem, never addressed an audience of more than one. He sought outlets for his massacre memoir, only to be rebuffed by publishers fearful of a racial reckoning. Here, Phillips' story is resurrected, and told in his words and on his time.

This is a first-person perspective on what happened in Tulsa in 1921 and why. It is one man's account, a subjective rendering with the advantage of vantage—with subtlety and nuance born of that perspective. It is a rare white telling of a horrific white taking (*i.e.*, a massacre perpetrated by a white mob), unfiltered, unadorned, and unvarnished.

Phillips, possessed of a photographic memory according to his son, Larry, vividly described what he variously refers to as a conflagration, a holocaust, and a calamity: "The rioting and burning mob rushed in and scattered over the Negro section of Tulsa like locusts attacking a field of grain, only it was more destructive. No tornado, earthquake, or other phenomena of nature ever destroyed a city in the USA so completely."

Most of the direct accounts of the massacre come from Black survivors. Seldom do the voices of white Tulsans emerge, and when they do, they mostly whisper. Phillips bellows. His words add to the whole, helping paint a fuller, richer portrait of what transpired, why, and to what end.

Phillips' original manuscript and the typewriter on which he composed it in the late 1960s and early 1970s are housed at Greenwood Rising, the new (2021), world-class Black Wall Street history center that sits on the southeast corner of Greenwood Avenue and Archer Street at the gateway to Tulsa's Historic Greenwood District.

Greenwood Rising offers four primary content galleries: (1) *The Greenwood Spirit*; (2) *Systems of Anti-Blackness*; and (3) *Changing Fortunes*; and (4) *The Journey to Reconciliation*. The primary goal of the facility is to immerse patrons in compelling history, stimulate them to think critically about that history and its relevance nation-wide, and galvanize individuals into action—into being change agents for a more equitable, just, and humane world. The man-uscript informs all these galleries, spanning some six decades of Tulsa history.

It is impossible to appreciate the scope and significance of the massacre without understanding what it destroyed and how those impacted responded. What was this "Greenwood District"—this "Black Wall Street?"

Early in the twentieth century, the African American commu-nity in Tulsa, Oklahoma, emerged as a nationally renowned center of black entrepreneurship. Legal segregation at the time limited the commercial options of African Americans. This economic de-tour—this diversion of dollars—spurred business development and economic prosperity in the black community. A talented cadre of African American businesspersons and entrepreneurs emerged.

Statesman and educator Booker T. Washington reportedly dubbed Greenwood Avenue, the nerve center of Tulsa's historic African American community, the "Negro Wall Street" for its pro-liferation of black businesses and the bustling business climate. Later in the twentieth century, "Black" replaced the then-dated term "Negro," and this storied community became known as "Black Wall Street."

On May 30, 1921, an elevator encounter between two teenag-ers, one black, the other white, in downtown Tulsa, lit the fuse that set Tulsa's African American community, the Greenwood District, ablaze.

Tulsa—already a tinderbox; a powder keg—reflected the na-tional context of racial strife and anti-Blackness. The rising tide of Ku Klux Klan engagement signaled and cemented white suprem-acy as the prevailing human relations philosophy.

Black successes and the material trappings thereof—home ownership, relative economic independence, and the objective manifestations of wealth (*e.g.*, automobile ownership, fashion, and leisure time activities) caused cognitive dissonance for seg-ments of the white community who felt themselves congenitally superior, and thus entitled to better lives than those of their Black contemporaries.

Even the land on which the Greenwood District set became the target of land lust—a desire by corporate and industrial types to seize the land for what they considered higher and better uses.

The media stoked racial discord. *The Tulsa Tribune* published a series of inflammatory, incendiary articles and editorial that raised the temperature on race relations in Tulsa.

Dick Rowland's alleged assault of Sarah Page triggered unprecedented civil unrest. Fueled by sensational reporting, particularly by *The Tulsa Tribune*, jealousy over black economic success, and a racially hostile climate in general, mob rule held sway.

Law enforcement officers deputized some of the white assailants. Mobs prevented firefighters from extinguishing the flames. In a span of fewer than twenty-four hours, people, property, hopes, and dreams vanished. The Greenwood District burned to the ground. Property damage ran into the millions. Hundreds of people died. Scores more suffered grievous injury. The assault on the Greenwood District left many African Americans homeless and destitute. Some fled Tulsa, never to return.

There would be no full accounting for the "Negro uprising." Murderous mobsters got off scot-free. Governmental units and white community and business leaders eschewed reparations. *The Tulsa Tribune* and, by extensions, at least some of its loyal readership, disparaged the prospect of rebuilding Black Wall Street.

Against the odds, black Tulsans regrouped and rebuilt. The Greenwood District rose from the ashes. Over the years, a host of social, economic, and political factors shaped the community's fortunes. Even today, the legacy of the 1921 Tulsa Race Massacre looms large in Tulsa.

Black Wall Street yet lives. Though no longer the Black economic and entrepreneurial mecca *a la* the early-to-mid-1900s, the community brims with possibility and promise.

The Greenwood District is experiencing a renaissance as a collaborative community rife with arts, education, culture, and entertainment. Greenwood Rising, the Greenwood Cultural Center, the Greenwood Chamber of Commerce, John Hope Franklin Center for Reconciliation, Oklahoma State University, Langston University, and ONEOK Field (home to the Tulsa Drillers minor league baseball team), join a host of small businesses, nonprofits, and historic churches in reclaiming part of the past glory of this special place.

Allow Phillips' account to transport you back to the Roaring Twenties; to 1921

Tulsa. Black gold flowed. Black pride swelled. Black entrepreneurship blossomed.

Imagine what it must have been like. Contemplate the difference race made. Consider, 100 years later, the extent to which race still makes a perceptible, palpable difference.

Hannibal B. Johnson, a Harvard Law School graduate, is an author, attorney, and consultant. He has taught at The University of Tulsa College of Law, Oklahoma State University, and The University of Oklahoma. Johnson serves on numerous board and commissions, including the federal 400 Years of African-American History Commission and the 1921 Tulsa Race Massacre Centennial Commission. His books, including *Black Wall Street 100: An American City Grapples With Its Historical Racial Trauma*, chronicle the African American experience in Oklahoma and its indelible impact on American history. Johnson's play, *Big Mama Speaks—A Tulsa Race Riot Survivor's Story*, was selected for the 2011 National Black Theatre Festival and has been staged in Caux, Switzerland. He has received copious honors and awards for this work and community service.

Content Warning

The publisher and editors of this book debated long and hard over language and usage. The original manuscript on which the book is based, written over a period of several years during the 1960s and 1970s and focused largely on events in 1921, contains epithets and other references now considered highly offensive. We ultimately concluded that publication of this work will aid in documenting the story of the 1921 Tulsa Race Massacre, and that the original language should be maintained as a written reflection of the attitudes and feelings of the times.

This book centers on a time in our history, decades ago, when the use of such language, though objectionable, was, in some circles, common. The most extreme example is the "N-word," which is used here only in direct quotations.

We in no way endorse or condone the use of such offensive language in a current context. We apologize in advance to anyone who may find the language upsetting or triggering.

Foreword

This is a true eyewitness account of one of the most tragic and horrible events that ever occurred in this nation. A mob of eighteen thousand people ran amuck, killed, and destroyed for seventeen hours. At least a hundred people were killed and about four hundred wounded. Homes, churches, schools, and business buildings were totally destroyed, leaving nine thousand homeless. More than half of the nine thousand were interned in jails and a baseball park. These of the other four thousand who were not killed or wounded, escaped by running cross-country to the hills and river or creek bottoms. Forced to leave everything they owned to the mercy of the mob and being homeless and destitute, hundreds kept going, never to return to Tulsa.

In no other incident since the Civil War have Americans inflicted such disastrous destruction and death on other Americans. And yet today, the danger of other horrible incidents developing into holocausts in which innocent people are sacrificed to satisfy the false pride and hatred of petty men increases daily.

Newspapers and television newscasts are filled with reports of confrontations in city after city, and even on ships of the armed services at sea. Most people will agree that the tragic mistakes of Kent State, Southern University,[1] and others should never have happened, but neither should the confrontations which brought them about. Not one thing can be listed as a gain from any of them. When miscalculation leads to violence, it is because the protest leaders fail in their responsibility to their followers and lack of knowledge in crowd control and mob psychology. Those who agitate and lead protests should never manipulate their followers into situations where they become victims of violence.

Murder In The Streets is a report on the results of a miscalculation by agitators who sent their followers to be slaughtered. Being curious as to why seventy-five armed men were marching down

7

the middle of the street, the writer followed them to the court-house where they demanded the release of a man from jail who at first was thought to be guilty of rape. The fact that he was innocent did not stop a town from being destroyed and hundreds of people from being killed or wounded.

The writer saw the first shot fired accidentally, which touched off the riot. Watching the terrible episode develop step by step and knowing how wrong the entire affair was has caused me to read about, study, and research riots and confrontations for years. Hopefully sharing this knowledge will help prevent others from becoming victims.

Also, the facts about how the most terrible riot in this nation's history developed have never been told. Each action by one group and counteraction by another will be examined and each rumor that added fuel to the fire will be reported. Included will be verbatim quotes of articles about the riot by six national magazines, and the results of the grand jury hearing reported.

The relevance of this narration is that the next confrontation could explode into a nightmare of death and destruction, and the writer asserts that this is the most complete coverage of a riot ever written.

Publisher's Note: This foreword was written more than fifty years ago, but the issues discussed remain the same today.

---

1. The author is referencing the Kent State shootings which occured on May 4, 1970, where four students were killed and the the November 16, 1972, shooting on the campus of Souther Univerity that resulted in the death of two students.

Chapter One

When conflagration rages out of control, and dozens of men are dead or dying with their blood forming rivulets in the streets and alleys, there should be no doubt about the reason for each death. A bullet from a rifle or pistol, or a blast from a shotgun was the actual cause of each death, but the reason for the shots being fired, and who was responsible, had to be determined by the grand jury. Killing without reason is murder.

Through the eyes of this writer, it will be possible for the reader to see the killings that were so senseless that they were unbelievable. The St. Valentine's Day Massacre in Chicago, by comparison, seems as tame as a shootout between blind men on a picnic. At least there were no innocent people involved in the Chicago murders. Those deaths were simply a climax to a gang war between two groups of hoodlums.

The killings in Tulsa, Okla., numbered approximately one hundred,[2] with several hundred wounded. Some so severely that they never completely recovered. Probably half of them were innocent bystanders. People who just happened to be at a place where irresponsible members of society ran amuck. With such a large number of dead and wounded, and property loss of more than two million dollars (by the values of today, about eight million)[3] it would seem that the reason for this all should be understood by everyone.

But it was not that simple. With some manipulation and agitation, an incident grew until it turned into a holocaust of fire and death.

One incident can be used by a careless, ignorant or vicious person to create another. That was the situation that brought the great explosion to its point of eruption. Rabble-rousers used one incident to create another, then used the two incidents to create a third *et cetera*. These tactics turned several incidents into one big event. Tied together like links in a chain conditions developed until a group of seemingly decent people changed into a raging mob of wanton killers.

Working hard, the agitators heated people up to such a feverish pitch that they didn't stop to think of the difference between an excuse and a reason. Actions of one group were met by counteractions by another until both sides turned into killers. Within a few hours, these tactics developed an extremely violent, rioting mob of fifteen to twenty thousand angry people.

This was certainly one of the most horrible manmade calamities that ever occurred in this nation. A city turned into ashes, and nine thousand people made homeless. The mob's lust for killing was satiated also, the dead and dying were everywhere. The rioting and burning mob rushed in and scattered over the Negro section of Tulsa like locusts attacking a field of grain, only it was more destructive. No tornado, earthquake, or other phenomena of nature ever destroyed a city in the USA so completely.

What could cause people to do such terrible things as to riot, kill, and burn? The causes are complex; agitators promote trouble because they are paid to, because they hate, or those who feel inferior like to talk big. And if aroused, the pioneering, frontier sort of people can become violent.

"Boomtown," sprang up over night during the days of the oil gushers in the southwestern section of the United States, and the largest and wildest "Boomer" of all was Tulsa. In late 1910, the population was around eighteen thousand and it was the largest town in that part of the state. A frontier sort of place in the heart of what was known as the Indian Nations Country. Composed mostly of the hardy pioneering sort of people, Tulsa had already known excitement, but nothing like that which came with the oil boom.

When it was learned that Tulsa was sitting on top of a huge oil field, the boom was on, and people came pouring in from everywhere. As the largest town in the vicinity, it became the center of the oil business and adapted itself almost completely to supplying the various needs of the oil and gas producers. Geologists, drillers, tool-dressers, pipe liners, teamsters, roustabouts, or rough-necks, as the laborers in the oil fields were called, came flocking into Tulsa in such numbers that it was difficult to find even standing room on the trains.

The supply and equipment companies brought more hundreds of people in as fast as they could find space to open their businesses. With the oil companies and the supply people scrambling for store and office space, and the town growing faster than houses and buildings could be built, work continued night and day, Shifts of oil field workers continued drilling oil wells around the clock, and carpenters, plumbers, painters, bricklayers, and electricians were replaced by another shift which worked at night on the store and office buildings. Bright floodlights were spotted around working areas permitting work to continue without interruption.

People stood in lines waiting for others to finish eating in cafes, restaurants, and hotel dining rooms. Barbershops gave numbered cards to their customers as they entered the shops, and they waited to be called for shaves and haircuts. Open night and day, they still seemed to always have waiting customers. Tulsa had become a booming metropolis overnight.

Along with the oil men and their workers, came the gamblers, the shady ladies of every size, shape, and color, and their pimps. Living space simply could not be built fast enough. Many hotels rented their rooms in shifts. Rooms were rented from six a.m. until six p.m. to a person that worked during the night, then from six in the evening until six in the morning to someone that worked days.

By 1915, the town was completely surrounded by oil wells. The population had climbed to sixty-five thousand and the oil fields had expanded from Tulsa County, into Creek, and Osage counties, making the Osages the wealthiest Indian tribe in the USA. The oil wells that lined both banks of the Arkansas River which runs through Tulsa, gushed thousands of barrels of oil each day.

The first oil strike was made a few miles south of town, and within five years it was found to be not only beneath the town itself but in every direction from the new "Oil Capitol." The great Cushing Field which included Drumright, and Oilton, all owned by Tulsa based companies, flowed millions of barrels of oil and poured hundreds of millions of dollars into Tulsa, also made the three smaller boomtowns wealthy. And while the Cushing Field, a few miles west of Tulsa was pouring forth "Black Gold," new strikes were being made north of town in the Osage Indian Nation.

New oil strikes were made a hundred miles southwest of Tulsa also. Then new boomtowns sprang up in the oil fields and grew from a few oil company workers into towns of five or ten thousand people within a year. Tulsa was the hub of the wheel, with spokes coming in from all directions. Equipment and supplies flowed out along these spokes to every new oil well that was drilled.

By 1921, with a population approaching ninety thousand, Tulsa officially became the "Oil Capitol" of the world. Deluxe hotels and office buildings with marble lobbies, were a part of the new scene. Large department stores and cosmopolitan type dress shops, catered to the "gals" and wives of the oil millionaires.

The famous Hotel Tulsa was filled to capacity the moment it opened for business. There is not a thing that can be said about this well-known hostelry, that would be an exaggeration. Before enough space in the new office building was available for all of the oil men, many conducted their business while sitting in the beautiful lobby of the hotel. Or they walked up the great white and gray marble steps to the mezzanine floor and sat in the large luxurious, sofas and chairs while they traded, bought, or sold, oil leases worth millions.

The writer now owns and lives on a small ranch thirty miles from Tulsa where Harry Sinclair made a rather large oil strike in 1918. A considerable amount of oil was produced from the 160-acre lease for several oil companies who bought and sold the place over the years. Many of the great oil and gas companies had their beginning in Tulsa. The Phillips 66 Company is one of those which grew to maturity on Oklahoma oil. Both of the Phillips brothers, Frank and Waite, were active in those early boomtown days in Oklahoma. Josh Cosden founded the Cosden Oil and Refining Company, which is today, the DX Company.

There had been at least a couple of dozen wealthy oil men that contributed greatly to Tulsa's growth and prosperity. Few donors in this nation have been in the class of Waite Phillips, He gave an almost new twenty-story office building that cost millions of dollars, to the Boy Scouts Of America. To make certain that there would always be room for outings and a place for boys to roam, he donated a large ranch worth more millions to the scouts. To the city Of Tulsa, he gave his home, a huge mansion with acres of beautiful grounds, and an art collection worth several million. The

Philbrook Art Center is one of the great art museums in the Southwest. The Philbrook Art Center, Philtower Building, and the ranch combined probably have a value of forty million dollars. Quite a donation, wouldn't you say?

Thomas Gilcrease, who was part Indian, spent a large oil fortune on western paintings, rare documents, and artifacts. Every painting by a top Indian artist that could be bought, regardless of cost, was added to the Gilcrease collection. A building was erected on some very valuable acreage in beautiful rolling hills of Osage County on the northern edge of the city limits, then Thomas Gilcrease gave acreage, buildings, and millions of dollars' worth of painting and art objects to the city of Tulsa. The Gilcrease Museum Of Art And Natural History is the greatest collection of Indian and western art in the world.

Tulsa University's Skelly Stadium is named for William Skelly, of Skelly Oil Company. A civic leader and donor of great value to Tulsa. The LaFortune family gave the city some extremely valuable land for a fine park and 18-hole golf course. And Tulsa University would not be the fine, beautiful institution that it is if the John Mabee family had not donated money for entire buildings on its campus. Also, the Oliphants are another family to whom Tulsa University owes many thanks.

There have been many more, but I have named only enough of the oil-wealthy people to show that there have been some real builders in Tulsa as well as those who put forth such a great effort to destroy an entire section of the city. Much like a person with a split personality, both good and bad, Tulsa had some of the finest builders and some of the worst destroyers ever seen in this nation. As proof that those who build are in greater numbers than those who destroy, Tulsa has grown and prospered. The booster spirit which began during the boomtown days caused the one-time prairie village to grow into one of America's most beautiful and modern cities with a population fast approaching half a million people. It has been said that those who know Tulsa well, never quite get over the love affair with her, and this I believe.

With so much going for it, I believe Tulsa was a happy town. It had booming prosperity with jobs for everyone. Signs in the windows of all barbershops, restaurants, grocery stores, and other businesses saying, "Help Wanted," and building contractors walking the streets asking men along the sidewalk if they knew any craftsmen in the building trades who wanted to work. The oil men were always hunting for drillers, tool-dressers, and other oil-field workers to start drilling new wells. Bootleggers were having a ball and selling anything that they could pour in a bottle. The "Shady-ladies," were running around with stockings full of money and ready to make more.

There were strong, progressive people building a city of the future. Thinking of their families, they built a community of beautiful churches, fine homes, and schools. Because of its location in a sort of frontier setting, many of Tulsa's citizens were of the pioneering breed. A rather proud, rugged, individualistic, kind of people.

On the other side of the coin, were some of the wildest, whooping, don't-give-a-damn persons imaginable. And hidden among the other citizens, most of whom were strangers to others, was the lawless element preying on the unwary, innocent, or weak members of the community. The old, old story, some make, and others take.

2. The exact number of people killed during the Tulsa Race Massacre are unknown and some estimates range as high as several hundred deaths.

3. The $6,000,000 figure would have been in 1979 and in today's money (2021) the amount would be in excess of $30,000,000.

Chapter Two

In an attempt to paint a picture of the young, fast-growing boomtown, it is necessary to use considerable space. Without some knowledge of the situation, it is not possible to understand how and why the terrible holocaust occurred. By highlighting Tulsa's background and the sort of people and conditions existing at the time, the reader can gain a better understanding of the how and why of the explosion.

When a convention was held in Tulsa it was usually a "Whing-Dinger." Everything that Tulsa did was on a grand and lavish scale. Known far and wide as the "OIL CAPITOL." it was felt that Tulsa had to out-do everything that was done by any other city of comparable size.

As a young spectator, I remember one parade which was so thrilling that the memory of it is still vivid after all of the years that have passed so kindly by me. The International Indian Convention brought Indians to Tulsa from all parts of the USA, Canada, and Mexico. All of the tribes of Oklahoma were represented. The boundaries of some of the Indian Nations joined at a spot where Tulsa is now located. Its city limits cover a part of what was once the tribal lands of the Creek, Osage, and some land of the Cherokee. These people were already here, all they had to do was get dressed in their beads and feathers and join the thousands of other Indians that came to the convention.

Thousands of parading Indians dressed in the most beautiful native costumes imaginable made that parade outstanding. They wore buckskins of all colors with scrolls of beadwork covering the costumes, armbands, and moccasins. Riding the finest pinto ponies and wearing great warbonnets of eagle feathers, they were a sight never to be forgotten.

There were Indian cowboys in the parade too. They chose to wear fine cowboy regalia instead of dressing in Indian costumes as they rode along as trail herders with their chuck-wagons. Some of the Indian cowboys rode pinto ponies also, but many rode prancing horses of Arabian ancestry.

Hotel Tulsa was the convention headquarters and although it had already seen more than its share of hubbub, it was never noisier, or uproarious than during the several days of the National Indian Convention. Expensive Persian rugs covered all of the areas where giant lobby chairs and sofas were located. Especially around the great white marble support columns which were spaced about sixty feet apart throughout the lobby. The support columns near the center of the great domed ceiling of the lobby were all surrounded by the rugs and large lobby chairs. Most hours of the day and into the night they were like little islands with people sitting and standing around chatting or talking business in groups.

To prove that the Indian riders could do more than just dress as cowboys, bets were made that one of the Indians bronc-busters could ride a wild horse in the hotel lobby. Ropes were brought in and wrapped around the marble columns from the first one to the next and so on until a corral was created with three strands of rope, the top rope near six feet high and the bottom strand three feet from the floor.

Gunny sacks were wrapped and tied around the horse's feet, and powdered resin was sprinkled around on the tile floor. They walked the horse up and down and around and around inside the rope corral which covered an area of sixty by one hundred and twenty feet. When the Indian leading the horse decided that it had been around enough to remember the size of the corral and get plenty of resin on the sacks, he signaled two other Indians to join him in the corral. One held the horse by the ear and its lower jaw while the third Indian took a firm grip on the bridle strap near the bit. He talked softly to the horse while patting its shoulder with his other hand.

Then the rider climbed into the corral wearing a pair of buckskin pants, boots without spurs, a beaded band around his head with one feather, but no shirt. As he walked over to the horse an argument started among the betting groups because the rider was not wearing spurs. Some said the horse would not buck as hard without spurs to gig him. The debate lasted a couple of minutes then everyone laughed at the no-spurs-trick, the Indian rider and his betting pals had pulled.

It developed that the only conditions agreed on when bets were made were that the horse must buck, and the rider stays on the horse for eight seconds, or until the horse stopped bucking. Nothing had been said about wearing spurs, nor had anyone specified that the rider could not pull leather. (Hang onto the saddlehorn with his hands) One of the Indians told the others that he owned a horse that was a light bucker unless he was gigged with spurs. But if spurred he would become a bawling, fishtailing, Wampus cat. The bronc-buster agreed to try that horse and his betting friends laughed long and loud believing that they had tricked the other bettors.

As did many other kids, when school let out for the summer this writer went job hunting. What a thrill! Hired as a relief operator at the Hotel Tulsa, I spent the next summer running the wealthy oilmen and other guests up and down in the elevators. It was from their conversations as they laughed and kidded with each other over five hundred-or-thousand-dollar bets, that I learned about the bronc ride that was to take place in the hotel lobby.

The Indian did ride the horse, but I don't believe he could have done it out on the solid ground. In spite of the sacks and resin, he slipped rather badly, but still gave the rider about all of the "buckin,' pitchin,' and sun-fishing," he could handle. The trick of riding the horse without spurs so he wouldn't buck so hard didn't work entirely to the satisfaction of the betting Indians, the rider had to hang on with his hands to finish the ride. The horse fell one time when its feet slipped from under him and the rider hit the floor hard, but as the horse scrambled to its feet the Indian hopped back in the saddle then managed to hang on for the required eight seconds. Those who were betting must have been satisfied, there were no lobby fights.

While the crowd which gathered around the corral during the bronc ride was yelling encouragement to either the horse or the Indian, there was another group of spectators watching the contest from the mezzanine. This may have been one reason why there wasn't any quarreling over the fact that the rider tumbled from the saddle when the horse hit the floor. A group of those who gathered along the marble railing on the mezzanine floor to watch the bronc ride began pouring corn whiskey from a five-gallon water bottle on the crowd below just as the gun sounded to end the ride. As the corn whiskey splattered over the people below, they began scrambling to get away from the spot beneath the whiskey bottle. Those not caught in the downpour around the corral, and the people lining the railing around the mezzanine floor yelled and laughed as if was the funniest thing in the world.

When I have mentioned the bronc riding incident to people who were not Tulsans, they have always been astonished. Some have attempted to be polite by trying to prevent their skepticism from showing as they asked, "Why would the hotel management permit such conduct? Surely that sort of thing damaged the reputation of the hotel. Why allow such a showy attractive place to be shattered and broken by those wild, rough people?"

The answer of course was money, lots of it. It was that sort of town. Any damage to the property would have been paid for immediately, and usually without a whimper. As unbelievable as it may seem, things of this nature were rather normal, conduct in boomtowns. And although Tulsa was booming quite a beautiful and modern young city, at heart, it was still a boomtown. Its rugged pioneering spirit gave it a sort of daring, "You can't live forever," attitude. The "take a chance," influence of the "wildcatter," pioneering oil men flowed strongly through early Tulsa.

To complete the picture of Tulsa at the moment the conflagration and killings occurred, one final brush stroke is added. One more incident that exploded with such tragic results will add to the understanding of those who profit from the mistakes of others. Hopefully, they avoid becoming similar victims.

Chapter Three

The Ku Klux Klan became a popular movement at the end of World War I. Having been dead or dormant since the reconstruction days following the Civil War, its revival caught on like a prairie fire and spread over the southern states like floodwaters. And to a lesser degree into the southwest. It even became strong in several north-central states, Illinois, and Indiana, in particular.

To complete the picture of the times, conditions, and the people of Tulsa at the time the tragic event exploded into a wild killing and burning night and day of horror, one episode of the Ku Klux Klan is added.

By early 1920, the Klan was in full-bloom and running roughshod over people in many states. It was never really strong in Tulsa, at least from the standpoint of numbers. It is doubtful if the membership ever grew to more than four thousand. Yet it held hood meetings. Burned crosses at night and scared the devil out of a lot of people.

Membership was restricted to persons twenty-one years of age or over, and since I was still in my teen years, I have no inside knowledge, yet I can vouch for one incident because it happened right in front of me. It was around seven o'clock on a Saturday evening when this writer along with more than a hundred other people saw some frightening evidence of the Klan's night-work. With the oil field work going on night and day, and many other businesses that never closed, there were throngs of people on the streets at all hours. Every day was like payday. All of the stores were open, and people were as busy as a hill of red ants, shoving their way in or out of stores carrying packages. Many of those who were not shopping were standing or milling around on the sidewalks in front of the stores as they waited for someone who was engaged in spreading the money around.

Automobiles were not bumper to bumper as they are today,

but Tulsa had more than its share of them. The cars, along with the heavy trucks as well as teams and wagons, created traffic problems during the peak hours of shift change or shopping periods and it was during such conditions that the incident occurred. Automobile horns sounded frequently as the drivers worked their way through the throngs of pedestrians at the street intersections.

Suddenly a car with horn blaring rolled through a crowd of people crossing the street and up to the entrance of the Robinson Building which was located on Main Street at the intersection with Third Street. A second automobile pulled to the curb behind it and both of them were loaded with men in white hooded robes. The back door of the first car opened and something was shoved into the street. Both cars then roared away as people standing along the curb gasped.

When people stepped back to open a path across the sidewalk to the building entrance, I saw a man wearing shorts only, but covered with a coat of tar and feathers rush through and into the building. He didn't wait for an elevator but bound up the stairs two at a time with several people running up the steps after him. A trail of dripped tar and feathers led to an office down the hall. Some of the people knocked on the door and asked if they could be of any help, but the office lights remained off and there was no answer. Indicating that the man wanted to be left alone, so most of us left and discussed the incident as we walked down the steps to the lobby.

One of my brothers was there also and recognized the man who had been tarred and feathered as he ran by. Later, he stated, "The man who had the tar on his body, is a bail-bondsman. I can't remember his name, but he is called 'Jew,' something or other. He makes bonds for people who have been arrested. I'll bet getting that tar off will be a lot harder than getting someone out of jail."

The next day the newspapers which had already been demanding that the police and sheriff's office stop the hooded night prowlers, really let go with both barrels at the Klan and the authorities because of the nighttime acts of terror. They reported that men had been whipped until their backs were bleeding. And that some of the victims whose flesh had been cut by thongs, then had warm tar and feathers painted and poured over their wounds. Some of the victims had also been ordered to leave town with threats of more severe whippings if they failed to obey, the news-papers stated.

Citizens were reminded by the newspapers that people were being judged and punished by Klan members whose only author-ity was hooded robes and whips. Then, people became aroused when the newspapers continued to demand action to stop the Klan from playing God, by acting as judge, prosecutor, and jury that has sat in judgment and delivered punishment.

Political pressure mounted because the public began to hold mass meetings and demand action. Detectives were assigned by police authorities to learn the identity of persons belonging to the Ku Klux Klan. And above all to determine if any police officers belonged to the organization. Sheriff's deputies were also warned that any of them found to be a member of the Klan, would be fired immediately.

With political pressure growing and people saying, "If some Klan members are not caught soon and sent to prison, some men in white robes are going to be found hanging from trees," no ef-fort was spared to stop the night-scourgers. So, the Ku Klux Klan quickly began to die an unlamented death.

The straw that really snapped the camel's back was the bold-ness of the Klan in dumping the bondsman in the middle of a crowd of people on a Saturday night. This alerted the public to the fact that the Klan and their acts of terror, were not just rumors.

Later, the newspapers reported the sin of the bondsman who had been whipped, tarred and feathered was that he made bond for some person whom the Ku Klux Klan members wanted to re-main in jail. The reports also stated that the bondsman had been told that every time he made a bond for a criminal, more severe whippings, tar, and feathers would be repeated until he was cured of making bond for people charged with crimes. And that if the whippings, tar, and feathers didn't cure him quick enough, a strong rope and a tall tree would stop him in a hurry.

If you are wondering what this has to do with the rioting mob which burned a city to the ground and killed with abandon, it will be revealed as having definitely played a strong role in the action. Fear and resentment can build, as did the condition leading up to the riot until one more straw on the proverbial camel, caused the disaster.

Chapter Four

Dusk was creeping over the city which the Chamber Of Commerce had at first tagged with the slogan, *The City With A Personality*, but which was now becoming better known as, *The Oil Capitol Of The World*. It could not truthfully be said that Tulsa, had started to settle down for a quiet peaceful evening because a quiet peaceful evening in Tulsa would have seemed like a rampage to most cities of comparable size.

The population of near eighteen thousand people in 1910 had swept upward with a hustle-bustle of activity to approximately eighty-five thousand by 1921. World War I had kept it from soaring above the hundred thousand mark, but when the war ended, Tulsa was off and running again, growing by several thousand each year. Oil was the black magic that worked its charm on the city that never slept. Since the first oil well just south of Tulsa began pouring money into the small town, other wells had gushed millions on top of millions of dollars worth of oil from the ground in and around the city. By 1921 many thousands of new people were a part of the Tulsa population seeking fortunes from oil.

This writer was one of five youngsters sitting on the steps of the old high school building singing barbershop harmony as twilight faded into dusk. The city's business district had almost surrounded the old school which was so small that many had to attend classes at elementary school buildings.

Standing in the center of a square block the old high school building was bounded on the west by Boston Avenue, on the east by Cincinnati, on the north by Fourth, and on the south by Fifth Street. A new ten-story office building was across Fourth Street north of the school, and across Boston on the corner at Fourth, the new telephone building was already occupied. Other new buildings were under construction and most of the homes to the south of the school had been torn down to make room for more new buildings. The entire area was in a constant state of flux, with old structures being torn down and new store and office buildings erected.

Having trouble finding just the right chords in our harmony arrangement of *Dear Old Girl*, we had sung it over and over before one of the fellows asked, "What do you suppose those men are doing with those clubs?"

He pointed across the school grounds to the southeast where a large group of men was walking south of Cincinnati. They had already crossed Fifth Street and were continuing south towards Sixth.

We stopped singing and turned our attention to the men that our baritone had pointed out. After a moment Harry said, "It is probably a chain gang. That must be brooms and shovels they are carrying."

The streetlights of that period shinned just bright enough to chase away some of the shadowy darkness of evening, but enough gloom was left to create a deceptive silhouette of things half-seen and half-imagined.

The men continued walking down the center of the street, two and three abreast. Then as the first few passed directly under the streetlight at Sixth Street, some of us began to doubt that those things carried in their hands and over their shoulders, were brooms and shovels.

Finally, after all of us had stared into the murky half lighted area at the marching men a few moments, Les offered, "That is not a chain gang, there must be seventy-five men in that group, and chain gangs never have more than twenty-five. Besides those things they are carrying look more like clubs than brooms and shovels."

Without another word, all of us started down the sidewalk from the school building to Fifth Street as we saw the group of men turn west on Sixth. We walked a half-block west in Fifth to Boston, then south to Sixth in time to see that it certainly wasn't a chain gang. City prisoners serving time for public drunkenness, disturbing the peace, and other minor crimes who couldn't pay their fines because they never worked were used to clean the streets at night, hence the name, chain gang.

Instead of shovels and brooms, the men walking west on Sixth

Street were all Negros, carrying rifles and shotguns. As the last of the men in the group began crossing Boston, we fell in beside them and while they marched down the center of the street, we walked west on the sidewalk, A few of the approximately seventy-five men did not have rifles or shotguns, instead, they carried revolvers.

We kept pace with them and whispered to each other as to what might be happening. The men in the street paid no attention to us as we walked along, speculating in whispers. From their actions, it appeared that we didn't exist. They walked west one block to Main Street, crossed over, and continued a half block to the county courthouse. Then they stopped and lined up in front of the Sixth Street entrance to the courthouse and county jail.

We walked up on the courthouse lawn with a few other people who had seen the lines of marching men crossing Main Street and followed in curiosity. Not more than a dozen or so were on the lawn at first, but people were gathering fast. Everyone was asking us what it was all about, and we were asking the same thing, but no one had an answer.

Several of the Negros held a conference out in the main body of their group but no part of their conversation carried to us up on the lawn. Finally, they seemed to reach a decision of some sort and broke up the huddle. When they returned to the others, information seemed to be passed up and down the rows of men gathered in the street. Then some were heard to say, "We'll do it, even if they don't like it, you tell 'em."

One Negro speaking louder than the others said, "Tell it to 'em straight out, tell it to 'em."

Our over-sized quartet of five people still hadn't found out what was happening but was still asking when a couple of men came out of the courthouse and stopped to survey the crowd. There were six gray stone steps above the sidewalk level and on each side of the steps were white marble balustrades[4] leading up to where the two men stood on the top step. A hush fell over the crowd gathered on the lawn and in the street when one man held up his arms for attention.

"I am the Sheriff of Tulsa County, " he said. "Now you men in the street listen to me. Go home before a lot of people get hurt. You have no business coming up here and parading around with these guns like that. If you are law-abiding people you will go home before some real trouble starts."[4]

One of the Negros shouted, "We'll go home when we get that Negro boy you all want to lynch." Several mumbled agreements.

The Sheriff replied, "No one is going to be lynched here. There is not going to be a charge against that young man. The white girl has admitted that he did not harm her. She said that she was nervous and scared, so she screamed when he grabbed her. That is all there is to the case. She is a very nervous person, but she is not going to press charges because no harm was done. Go home now, I give you my word that Richard will be released in the morning."

Some of the Negros were not satisfied. "If there is no charge, why don't you turn him over to us now?" one of them asked with hostility.

"That's right, we can take him now, so let us have him?" another demanded.

"I can't release him tonight, it isn't possible," the Sheriff answered.

"Why not? If there ain't no charge, why can't you let us take him?" another voice asked.

A Negro shouted belligerently. "And if we leave him here he's a goner. They'll hang him high as Judgment Day."

"Listen to me," the Sheriff shouted, "No one is going to hang anybody from this jail! But I can't turn him over to you tonight for two reasons; first, only a judge can release a person once he has been charged with a crime. When I said there would not be a charge, I meant that it will be dropped in the morning. The city police arrested the young man and transferred him to the county jail for safekeeping until the investigation was over. When the girl admitted that she was so scared that she might have made a mistake as to Richard's intentions, that ended it. He will be released in the morning!"

The Sheriff was winded from yelling to be heard. Hesitating momentarily to grab a breath of air, he continued, "The second reason I can't release him is that we can't give in to lawlessness. Mobs are not going to run this town. So, go home before trouble starts."

The men in the street discussed the situation for a few moments, then, with the cooler heads prevailing, they all turned slowly and headed back in the direction from which they had arrived.

I noticed that the courthouse lawn had filled with people and they were overflowing into the intersection of Sixth and Boulder, the first street west of the courthouse. Every new arrival crowded in to ask someone what was happening. We were glad to tell everyone that would listen what we knew about the exciting affair. The feeling of importance made it almost as much fun as singing harmony. Perhaps not more than thirty people had been there at the beginning of the incident, having seen and heard it, we told it all.

Suddenly someone said, "Look, the Negros are coming back!"

It was true, they were coming up to fill the street in front of the courthouse again. Only this time there seemed to be more than there had been in the first group. (Later it was learned that those returning home from the courthouse had met another group on their way up there and were talked into going back.) There had to be considerably more men in the second bunch because the two groups combined totaled at least two hundred Negros as they lined up in front of the courthouse entrance.

Again, the Sheriff came out and stood on the top step. Two other men were with him this time, one was a Negro. After surveying the large crowd a few moments, the Sheriff asked, "Why did you come back here? I advised you to go home before trouble started that we couldn't control, why are you back?"

"Because we don't believe you when you say that boy will be protected," one of the Negros answered.

Before the Sheriff could reply, another one shouted, "You may not have him in your jail right now. We were told that you have probably already turned him over to a mob of lynchers!"

The Sheriff attempted to answer and was again cut short by yet another shouter, "You didn't do such a good job of protecting that other man that was hung a few months ago did you?"

Then other voices joined in with, "That's right, if you are such a good protector how come he got lynched?" And "You sure let him get hung, didn't you?"

This was in reference to the lynching of a white man whose name was Roy Belton, eleven months earlier. Belton had been arrested for the extremely brutal murder of a taxicab driver and was being held in the county jail awaiting trial on the charge. The murder trial never took place because Belton was taken from the jail by a mob and hanged.

Rumors were that several men who had special deputy sheriff's badges and commissions were allowed to move freely around the sheriff's office and jail, took advantage of this fact, and blocked the view of the jailers so the mob could swoop in and take over long enough to drag Roy Belton from the jail and hang him.

I will not dwell on the details of this episode because it had no connection to the incident then taking place between the Sheriff and the group of Negros, except that since the Negros cited the Belton lynching at the courthouse, it can be seen as coal-on-the-fire. It is certainly reasonable to think that agitators who organized the two groups of men that marched up to the courthouse, used the Belton lynching to excite the people in the Negro district. And since Richard Rowland was being held in the same jail from which Belton had been dragged by the mob, it is a fact that mentioning the comparison of Rowland being in that same jail would have caused fear for his life. Any agitator worth his salt as a troublemaker would never let such an opportunity pass.

One other phase of the Belton lynching taught a lesson about the morbid nature of a large segment of the population that I have forgotten. Many people are so afflicted with an abnormal, morbid curiosity that they will go to any length to secure a souvenir from the scene of some horrible disaster. The more terrible the tragic incident is, the more determined they become to gain a memento of the occasion.

The person who obtained the rope with which Roy Belton was hung, circulated around through the downtown area selling pieces of the rope for fifty cents an inch. The hanging took place in the early evening and it seemed that during the night, hundreds of people were walking around with pieces of rope measuring from one inch, up to a foot or more. I heard it said that it must have been the longest rope that ever hung a man. One man commented, "If all of the pieces of rope that have been sold as the hanging rope, were laid end-to-end, it would be more than a mile long.

The confrontation between the Sheriff and the Negroes continued with little to indicate that a peaceful agreement could be reached. He explained that the lynching of Belton had caused a change in the system, that nothing like it could ever happen again.

The Negros in the street were not convinced. One of them who had been a spokesman several times before said, "We are going to see if Dick Rowland is still in your jail. If he is, we are going to take him out. You said that white gal done lied about him, so we are goin' to take him away then we'll know that he is safe."

The Negro man standing beside the sheriff, probably a deputy sheriff, stepped forward and said, "Now man I tell you that Rowland is safe in jail. I am one of you and when I tell you that he is in jail and safe, you can trust me."

"The hell we can. You will say whatever the Sheriff tells you to say," a discordant voice yelled from the street.

Then another member of the Negro group shouted, "We're goin' to look for ourselves and if he's in there, we're goin' to take him home!"

A third voice added, "And if he ain't in there, we'll burn down this damn courthouse."

Others murmured agreement as yet another voice joined in with, "He's right. If Rowland is not in the jail, we'll set the whole damn place afire. That is, we'll set 'er afire and burn 'er down."

The Sheriff continued to shout until he had their attention. "Just a minute! Listen to me! No one is going to come into this building and take anybody out of jail. Make up your minds to that right now. There are more than twenty-five deputies standing at the window on those floors above."

He pointed to the upper floors where the courtrooms and jails were located, "Every one of those deputies has a rifle or shotgun ready to shoot the first person that tries to force his way inside. Look up at those windows. See those gun barrels pointing down at you? They will cut down the first man that makes a move to take over. Go home before a lot of people get shot. I am trying to keep someone from being hurt or killed, so go home."

I looked up at the windows indicated by the sheriff and although all of the courtrooms were dark, two or more gun barrels could be seen pointing towards the street from each window. Since the lights were off it was simply not possible to see how many men there were in the dark, but the guns were certainly there and pointed towards the Negros.

"I told you before that the attempted rape charge would be dropped in the morning." The Sheriff told the Negros as he began to repeat what he has said to the first group that came to demand Richard Roland's release. "The young girl has admitted that she might have misunderstood what Rowland was trying to do. She has signed a statement saying that she was nervous and scared and that when he grabbed her, she believed that he was trying to rape her, so she screamed."

The crowd on the lawn and the Negros in the street listened quietly as the Sheriff continued to relate the same things he told the first group of Negros and the small crowd of about thirty people gathered on the lawn trying to learn what the seventy-five Negros were doing there.

"The girl operated the elevator in the building where the incident occurred, and stated that Roland entered the elevator and stepped up so close to her that she became nervous and scared. There was no one else in the elevator and yet he came so close that he stepped on her foot and she slapped him. She said that he grabbed her, and she screamed just as the elevator stopped at the ground floor. She reported that she was still screaming when a man came rushing up and Rowland ran. She now admits that it might have neem as Rowland states, that he grabbed her because she slapped him."

The lawn was now covered with people and more coming up all the time.

Ending his explanation, the Sheriff admonished the approximately two hundred Negros, "Now, you people have no business coming up here with those guns. Parading around with those guns is against the law. Violence is easy to start, but hard to stop. Go home before a lot of unnecessary killing gets started."

As the Sheriff finished, a man dressed in some sort of uniform, I am not positive, but I believe it was a city traffic officer, stepped forward from the lawn and said, "Come here and put those guns in a pile by the curb."

He pointed to a spot near the lawn. When none of the Negros moved, he continued, "Come on, bring them here. You have no business with guns, they will only get you in trouble."

No one seems inclined to obey, so he stepped to the nearest Negro and took a rifle from his hand. Then to the next one and took a weapon from him also. He continued from one to another taking guns as he told them, "Come on now, hand over those guns before a lot of people get hurt. You can come back here and get the guns when trouble is over."

When he had eight to ten guns in his arms he walked to the curb and deposited them in a pile and went back for more. He took a second armload and left them in the same spot and returned to start over when the fuse to the powder keg was ignited.

Seemingly puzzled as to what to do about the uniformed man taking their weapons, the Negros were still lined up in the street waiting when it happened. I do not recall a movement by any of the people on the lawn, nor had any of the Negros attempted to leave or resist. Everyone stood spellbound and all eyes were on the man in uniform.

The officer was saying, "You don't want to get into trouble do you? Why don't you put those guns by the curb like good citizens?" as he walked over to a rather large Negro man and took hold of a shotgun. Instead of releasing it, the Negro jerked it free and turned to run. He had taken not more than two steps when the officer caught and again grabbed the shotgun. They struggled over it for a moment. Then while they tugged back and forth with the gun barrel pointed skyward, a shot was fired into the night air.

Flames shot from the end of the barrel and a loud roar shattered the semi-quietness of the night. Then followed a second or two of total silence before, to quote the Sheriff in a later statement to the newspapers, "All hell broke loose. Guns barked and lead flew from rifles, shotguns, and revolvers in all directions. People fell mortally wounded on the lawn and in the street. It was the most senseless thing I ever saw."

Like everyone else, I watched the officer wrestle with the Negro man over the shotgun. When the flame erupted from the gun followed instantly by a loud blast, I was stunned into a second of confused inaction. But when a second shot "boomed" from the barrel of a gun, I hit the ground and scrambled over against the marble balustrade[5] by the steps faster than a "prairie dog" can flop into his hole. Seeing the flames from the guns in the darkness and hearing roaring blasts, sent a shot of adrenaline from my suprarenal glands saying, "Move now and think about it later" and I did.

Rifles and pistols popped or cracked, and shotguns boomed in a continuous rhythmic pattern for a few seconds. Then like a string of firecrackers, they fizzled to an occasional pop. When the shooting stopped I tried to crawl from under a pile of people but had to wait for some of them to roll off before I could get to my feet. When able to squirm free of the smothering weight of the eight or nine people, I was struck by the horror of the scene.

People were down on the lawn. Some were moaning and trying to crawl away. Others lay still in death. A couple of people nearest the sidewalk were almost blown into shreds by shotgun blasts at close range. A moment after the shooting started the Negros broke and ran in all directions, but as they scurried toward the darkness, they left several of their members dead or dying where they had fallen in the street. Some headed for the alley beside the courthouse but never made it. Shots from a group of white men in the alley and on top of the courthouse brought them down. It is doubtful that any of the Negros ever dreamed that such an ending would result from their armed incursion of the courthouse area, so when the shooting began they tried to get as far as possible from that place.

The shooting probably lasted not more than eight or ten seconds, but to this writer, it seemed an eternity. Then all that remained as an aftermath of man's stupidity, was the dead bodies and the moaning and groaning of the wounded. Off in the distance, an occasional shot rang out, a reminder of man's killer instinct. The thin veneer of civilization was scratched, and men reverted to the same wolf-pack killers as the ancestry. Now around the courthouse were dead bodies, and both black and white people were hurt and moaning and pleading for help.

My harmony-singing friends joined me as they came from places of concealment behind the balustrade and nearby shrubbery. Then ambulances arrived and men climbed out in a hurry and went to the side of those who were moaning with pain. Quickly they began placing the badly wounded people on stretchers. Those who could walk were helped to stagger to the ambulances. A couple of doctors appeared and began administering to the wounded.

There was nothing that we could do to assist anyone, so we stayed back out of the way and watched the doctors and ambulance drivers while discussing the situation. Now and then as they examined the people who were down on the lawn or in the street, they indicated that there was one that could be left until later. No time to worry about the dead, until those that could be saved were cared for.

Men had gathered from the alley by the side of the courthouse and from the one across the street. They were joined by others who had climbed down from the roof of the courthouse and other buildings. We learned that dozens of armed men had followed the fleeing Negros as they ran toward every dark spot they could see. Most of the Negros headed for the darkness then made a wide circling movement to avoid the brightly lighted business district as they hurried back toward their section of town.

We were surprised to learn that there were two or three hundred white men who were heavily armed, surrounding the courthouse when the shooting started. Several of them said that they had joined the curious crowd on the lawn when the first group of Negros came to the courthouse. After listening a few minutes, they realized that trouble was brewing and slipped away to hurry home for a gun.

When they returned, they did not rejoin the crowd that was still gathered on the lawn. Instead, they climbed to the courthouse roof in the darkness, or hid in the alley and waited. Others said that they had a rifle or shotgun in their parked car and hurried to get it. When they returned they joined those that were already hidden in the darkness.

4. The Tulsa County Sheriff was Willard "M.C." McCullough during the 1921 Tulsa Race Massacre and was heavily criticized for his actions or lack of action.

5. A balustrade is a vertical moulded shaft, square, or lathe-turned form found in stairways, parapets, and other architectural features.

Chapter Five

At the Royal Theatre, located at Main and Fourth streets, it was near time for the last vaudeville show of the night to start. The number two motion picture operator was a regular member of our singing group, and when the last stage show was over, it was the end of his day. The other operator was also a regular member of our singing group, when the last stage show was over, it was the end of his day. While the other operator worked at getting the film ready for the last showing, our twenty-year-old friend ran the spotlight for the last vaudeville show. Intending to meet him at the end of his shift anyway, it was now more important, for we had some exciting news that was aching to be told.

We left the courthouse about 9:30 p.m. and walked the half block to Main, then turned north toward Fifth Street. Strolling along discussing the excitement of the evening, our attention was suddenly attracted to the loud roar of an automobile coming toward us from about a block south. The driver had the car's motor wide open and was creating a deafening noise. As we turned to look in that direction, flames shot from the barrel of a shotgun which was pointed toward the west side of the street. No one lingered to see who, what, or why, the shot was fired. Like a covey of quail, we scattered in every direction.

There were twenty-five or thirty other people walking along in that block. So, the scrambling for doorways that were deep enough to offer some protection, was frenzied. A couple more shots were fired down the street before an automobile with ten or twelve Negros in it swept past the entrance to the building where some of us had taken refuge. Two members of our group were several paces ahead of the rest of us and consequently had found shelter in another location. However, several other people were nearby and rushed back in the deep shadowy doorway with the rest of us when the roaring car and gun blast sent everyone scrambling for safety. (Later we learned that our two friends were near the intersection and scooted around the corner.)

Maybe the Negros in the speeding car were firing shots into the air, or into the front window of a store because we never heard of anyone being wounded or killed in that block, but windows were shot out of many places on Main Street. If they only wanted to scare or shake people up, they darn sure succeeded.

Finally venturing out of our hiding place as did others who had sought shelter in building entrances, we looked for our friends, but without success. (When they turned the corner they kept going, headed for home, believing that we would have sense enough to do the same).

Not finding them and believing that they would go to the theatre where we were supposed to meet our singing operator friend, the three of us headed there while keeping a wary eye open for speeding cars loaded with Negros.

Nearing Fourth Street, the first theatre we came to was the Majestic, a deluxe motion picture house where I had worked as an usher one summer, and still worked in relief occasionally on a weekend, or evenings if someone was ill. Only a small narrow building housing George's Fruit Store separated the Majestic from the Royal Theatre at Fourth Street. And although the Royal was on the corner with the stage door opening onto Fourth Street near the alley, its lobby, like the Majestic was on Main Street.

Hesitating a moment to glance at the upcoming picture display, I waved greetings to the cashier then joined my two friends in front of the fruit store. Glancing into the store where several people were buying stuff to nibble on, it seemed appropriate to remark that, "come-hell-or-high-water" some people would have to have something to chew on.

Things seemed normal causing us to forget for a moment the happenings of the evening. But the reminder was sudden. Two automobiles came speeding down Main Street and since they were running quietly without the eardrum-shattering noise of blaring horns and roaring cutouts, they were almost beside us before someone shouted, "Look out! Two cars loaded with Negros coming up fast!"

With only a fleeting glance toward the two cars, I leaped toward the deep lobby of the Royal Theatre. In addition to my two friends, several other persons who were looking at the posters and photos in front of the theatre and those who were nearby on the streets dashed into the lobby for safety.

Rushing on, we were just reaching the doors at the end of the long lobby when the roar of shotguns and the sound of shattering glass induced an extra burst of speed that sent us hurtling through the doors, past the ticket taker, and into the inner foyer like a gang of blockers out ahead of a ball-carrying halfback. Our momentum was halted by a violent crash into a howling, fighting mob of several hundred frightened people.

Screaming, and clawing their way up the aisles and into the lobby they shoved us back toward the street. Realizing that it was useless to push back at them and lucky enough not to be knocked down and trampled by the violently frantic mass of people, I rolled along with them until I could slide off to the side.

The mob action was set off when several men chased a Negro man down the alley in back of the theatre and out onto Fourth Street where he saw the stage door and dashed inside. Seeing the open door, the Negro rushed in and hurried forward in the darkness hunting a place to hide.

Suddenly he was out on the stage in front of the picture screen and blinded by the bright flickering light coming down from the operator's booth in the balcony. After shielding his eyes for a moment, he regained his vision enough to locate the steps leading from the stage down past the orchestra pit to the aisle just as the pursuing men rushed onto the stage. One of them saw the Negro and yelled, "There he is, heading for the aisle!" As he finished the sentence a roaring blast from a shotgun dropped the Negro man by the end of the orchestra pit.

Unaware of what had been happening outside during the evening, the audience nevertheless knew that they were seeing something that was not a part of the show and panicked. They began clawing, screaming, and fighting to get out of that place. Bursting out into the lobby, many of the violently agitated people were so excited that they failed to realize that they were already outside and continued to push, shove, and scream.

Almost knocked down several times, I finally rolled free and crossed the sidewalk where Harry and Dewey joined me. We noticed that the plate glass was gone from the fruit store window.

That accounted for the shattering glass sound which followed the roar of the shotgun as we rushed into the theatre.

Not realizing that our two friends that we had lost a few minutes earlier had sense enough to decide that Main Street was no place for peaceful, law-abiding citizens, we continued to look for them among the huge crowd that grew larger by the minute.

A few moments later we hailed the singing operator as he came out of the theatre. Before we could relate what had happened within the last couple of hours, he told us what had set off the riot in the theatre. The milling crowd continued to grow until the street in front of the theatre and the intersection at Fourth and Main were filled with people. Hundreds poured into the street when the manager of the Majestic decided to close for the night.

To be free of the jostling crowd we moved to about a hundred feet west of Main, on Fourth Street, and began discussing the many incidents that had happened during the evening. Soon we barely had elbow room there as more people arrived. Everyone discussed the exciting experiences that they had been involved in or witnessed.

Then some more horrible action occurred almost in front of us. Hearing a yell, we looked in that direction and saw a Negro man that had burst from the alley across the street and was running along the north side of Fourth, toward Main Street. Several men rushed out of the alley and one of them raised a rifle to shoot the Negro but two of the others shoved the barrel down toward the pavement. The shot would have been toward the huge crowd on Main.

Someone shouted, "Look out, the Negro has a gun!" Most of us had seen the rifle by then and were looking frantically for something to crawl in or under. Then suddenly a Cadillac car came speeding down the crowded street and with horn blasting and tires squealing, it swerved over toward the Negro man just as he arrived across the street from us and a young woman poked a shotgun out the window and fired a blast into the Negro. The distance was less than twenty feet and as the Negro man dropped and rolled over near the curb, the man driving the Cadillac gunned it and went flying off toward the darkness.

In seconds a large crowd gathered around the fallen man who had been shot in the face and chest. He was bleeding so badly that if it had not been for his hands, it would have been impossible to tell if he was black or white.

An ambulance rolled up and two men hopped out and began asking the crowd to step back and permit them to put the man on a stretcher. They must have been cruising nearby, for no one could have called them that quick. The crowd opened a path barely wide enough to allow the ambulance men to lay the stretcher beside the victim.

As they prepared to put him on it, a very large man who had picked up the rifle that had fallen from the Negro's hand and skidded against the curb, said, "Hold it. Don't touch him. There are a lot of people who have been hurt and need you. Go find some of them."

"Why not this one? He needs us too, doesn't he?" One of the men asked.

The man with the rifle answered, "Because he is a nigger and was up here hunting trouble. Maybe he shot some of the white men that are dead or dying, go hunt some of them."

The ambulance driver hesitated a moment as if undecided, so the big man jabbed the rifle into his stomach, "Get goin' in a hurry or join him with a bullet in the guts. Decide in a hurry, which is it?"

The men hopped in the ambulance and left in a hurry. But it wouldn't have made any difference to the Negro any way, he was already dead. It was around 10 p.m. when we walked away from the crowd surrounding the dead Negro. Harry was the first to speak, "Well, I guess it is all over now. That must be the end of the trouble."

"I don't know," one of the fellows replied, "it seems to me that there is a huge crowd of people on the streets and none of them appears to be in a hurry to leave. With a crowd of this size and many half-drunk, who knows?"

We walked up to Main Street and started to cross to the south side of Fourth while keeping a wary eye on the surroundings even though it hardly seemed possible that there could be more Negros left in the central part of town. But there certainly were a lot of white people running around with guns and some of them were plenty foolish as the man had proven when he pointed the rifle towards the crowded intersection.

But it did seem to be over, for any of the Negros who had not made it back to their side of town were never going to make it. We were strolling along just south of the Majestic Theatre when an Osage Indian friend drove by, then seeing us he pulled to the curb and the four of us climbed into his car. On a date at his girlfriend's home, he had not heard of the exciting incidents until now. He soon learned all that we knew.

I have known many people who had an appreciation for music, and yet, "Couldn't carry a tune in a basket." Our Osage friend went far beyond that. He couldn't sing a lick but would sit as still as a "pointer as a covey of quail," just listening. He was a true lover of quartet harmony. Besides being a good listener, (by our standards) he had quite a lot of money and a car. From an oil money family, he was twenty-years-old, and a very popular member of our crowd.

After driving up and down and around and around through the business section for a while discussing the happenings of the night I suggested that we drive down by the river and finish working out our harmony arrangement of *Dear Old Girl*. But Harry said, "I would rather drive out by the nurses' home, Or the girls' dormitory at the college and serenade them."

A rather frequent diversion of ours, but it seemed that tonight, none of the others were in the mood to sing. Then one of the fellows said, "I don't think I could get in the spirit for revelry without a couple of drinks. After all that has happened, a drink or two might not be a bad idea."

No one else suggested doing anything about that and since we had already parked on Main Street, we just sat there. Several thousand people were milling around on the streets as if waiting for something to happen.

Then two men stopped and leaned down to say to us, "We are deputizing groups of men with automobiles to patrol the streets that separate the white and Negro sections of town. We want to be certain that some black men do not sneak over and rape and kill a lot of white women during the night."

None of us said anything, too puzzled to answer I guess. So, one man continued with, "We want you men to patrol North Boston from Archer to Pine Street. Or if you would rather, take Cincinnati from Archer to where it dead-ends at the foot of Standpipe

Hill."

Again, none of us replied, probably because only the Osage who owned the car could agree. While he thought it over he continued, "Now don't let anyone get hurt up there. If you see anything suspicious get down here fast while blowing your horn. A thousand men will be ready to help in a minute."

This time they didn't wait for an answer, they turned and walked down the street to the next automobile. When they stopped to talk to the people sitting in it, Harry said, "I'm going down there and listen to what they say to those men."

"It was the same thing they said to us." He reported when he returned. "Those men agreed to patrol Cincinnati until daylight," he informed us.

There was no comment for several minutes, then Dewey asked, "Well are we going to do it or not?"

I was somewhat worried about the situation and since no one else answered, I stated, "We don't know who those men were. I thought a person had to take an oath of some kind and be twenty-one years old to be a deputy sheriff. How do we know that they have the right to deputize us? And Harry is the only one of us that is twenty-one years of age."

"Doesn't a deputy sheriff have to do what he is told? And if we don't do it will we get in trouble?" Dewey asked.

"I think we are more apt to get in trouble if we do it," I replied.

"I don't think there will be any trouble if we do, or don't do it," Harry answered. "All we have to do is decide if we want to patrol or not," he added.

Then someone remembered that we didn't have any sort of firearm, and we discussed this for a while before deciding that we probably wouldn't need one. Finally, the Indian said, "We were not told to go up there and shoot things up. All we were asked to do was to patrol the streets between the black and white section of town and if we saw anything that looked suspicious we were to rush back here and report it."

I suppose one might say that we were like most young people, (not prone to turn down a chance for excitement) for we went to patrol North Boston. Several times we drove up to Pine Street and back down Archer before starting to sing our unfinished arrangement of *Dear Old Girl*. Our Osage Indian driver cruised along listening while passing Standpipe Hill. Then a few blocks north of there, he turned over to Cincinnati on to Pine. The first three streets east of Boston ended at the south side of the hill but started again where it leveled off to the north.

Content to sing and leave the driving up to the Osage, we were not aware when he again turned at Pine and headed towards Archer once more. Completely engrossed in singing the right chords in our "Barbershop" style harmony, we had momentarily forgotten the tragic event that had occurred at the courthouse. But our forgetful state of mind didn't last long.

Abruptly our singing stopped, and we lost interest in hunting for the "Last Chord." Our driver jammed on his brakes and brought the car to a sudden stop and all of us began a mad scramble to pile out of the doors on the west side of the car. One moment of confusion, then the frenzied struggle to get out of there began, for we realized that we had been shot at.

A bullet "whanged" into the east side of the automobile striking a door-glass that was only partly rolled down. Almost before the driver could bring the car to a complete stop, most of us were out on the west side of it, and by the time he rolled out some of us were already crawling under it.

The shot came from the darkness of Standpipe Hill, so named because the water tower on top of the hill was the source of pressure for Tulsa's water system.

The playground of Sequoyah School ended at the foot of Standpipe hill about two hundred feet east of Boston Avenue. The school building and its grounds covered most of the area at the foot of the hill, the rest of the land for a considerable distance on either side of the school was vacant. The tall water tower was located a couple of hundred feet from the edge of the steep bluff, above the playgrounds.

From Archer Street, the land sloped upward gradually for several blocks, then abruptly leaped into the air to form the hill. Since there were few houses in the vicinity and Cincinnati, Detroit, and Elgin streets dead-ended at the foot of the hill on the south, the steep cliff with its lone water tower on top, loomed as a very spooky place at night.

During the first few seconds after that bullet struck the car our thoughts were darn sure not on the contour of the land, or dead-ending streets. I am certain that with one accord, we were wishing that we were out of that place.

We were still hugging the west side of the automobile tighter than paint on a wall a couple of long minutes later when another car loaded with men who had also been patrolling Boston, rolled up. Its headlights outlined our car in the middle of the street with the five of us either under or crouched against it. A voice yelled, "Do you need help? What is the trouble?"

"Hell yes," Harry replied. "But turn off your light there is a sniper on the hill. He just shot the glass out of the door on the east side of our car and he may still be on the hill."

The driver turned off his lights, but instead of jumping out of the car, he gunned it. They were two blocks down the street when the lights were turned on again. The driver must have had his foot rammed halfway to the gas tank because the car was really traveling away from there.

We waited a minute to see if there would be a second shot, but none came. Then we decided to get out of there, and that we did. With speed, haste, dispatch, alacrity, and all that sort of stuff we dove into the west side of the car faster than any litter of pigs ever went to a feed trough. As we piled in on top of each other, on the floor on in somebody's lap, our driver yelled, "Shout when you are ready to go!"

Harry answered, "Get the hell out of here and don't spare the gasoline!"

And it didn't take nearly as long for us to decide to stop patrolling as it had taken to start it. Many things were mentioned that were not discussed before beginning the patrol. One of the fellows remembered that his parents hadn't been notified that he was staying out a little late. Another one said, "I should go by home and let the family know that I'm all right."

I stated that if I went home it would be all but impossible to get out again. Someone suggested that if we phoned our homes to state that we were going to sing a little while, but would be home soon, any worry would be removed. Deciding to handle it that way, we headed for a telephone and a waffle at one of the better known restaurants. Believing that the excitement was over, we were content to just sit and talk about it for a while.

We saw drunks staggering along the streets hanging onto

half-empty bottles and now and then one would face skyward and scream and whoop as loud as possible. Instead of the crowds on the streets diminishing as the hours passes, they grew larger. A great many of those people lining the sidewalks were holding a rifle or shotgun in one hand and grasping the neck of a liquor bottle with the other. Some had pistols stuck in their belts.

Chapter Six

One of the most popular places in Tulsa, the restaurant was usually crowded. But that night it was not just crowded, it was packed with people from wall to wall. They were standing along the walls waiting for those who were seated at the counters to leave, then everyone nearby joined in the scramble for the vacated stool. Also, in the back of the place, people were jammed together like crowder peas.

Rumors were a dime-a-dozen. Also, some information thought to be rumors, later were found to be true. We learned that five white people were killed during the shoot-out at the courthouse. Also, that more than a dozen were wounded, some so serious that they might die before morning.

Approximately a dozen Negros had been killed at the courthouse or around the business section as they tried to escape. I saw some of them fall on Sixth Street at the courthouse and the one on Fourth. And heard about the one on Third Street and in the Royal Theatre. Also, that two were killed in alleys and two others died in the battle on Boulder Avenue.

With approximately twelve killed and forty wounded, a fourth of the armed group that went to the courthouse demanding Richard Rowland's release and threatening to burn the building if their demands were not met, were either dead or wounded and Rowland was still safely locked in the county jail. What a tragic episode, and yet it was a mere beginning.

One of my brothers witnessed the killing of two people that night. The first one was evidently one of the Negros attempting to escape from the courthouse area. It happened at Third and Main streets at approximately the same time we saw the man blasted with a shotgun on Fourth Street. He stated that a large Negro man came running east on Third, evidently escaping from the shootout that took place on Boulder Avenue a block west, or from the alley west of Main Street. Running hard, he came toward my brother who was standing on the east side of Main. He had almost reached the curb when a young man (my brother guessed that he was about seventeen) stepped from the crowd watching the Negro approach and slammed two shots from a rifle into him before he hit the pavement. When examined a few seconds later, he was dead.

A crowd swarmed around the young man who then pulled off his shirt and said, "Look! This is what they did to me in the Negro section just about dark!"

His shirt was a bloody mess as he exposed his back which had been lashed so hard that large welts were still raw and bleeding.

"The young man whose face was badly swollen explained that he was a messenger and went to the Negro section to deliver a telegram. He was grabbed by about thirty Negros, beaten, kicked, then tied to a post and whipped with a piece of wire. Then they untied him and told him to come back over here and report what happened to white people who came to their town," my brother stated. He continued the explanation with, "His lips were so badly split and swollen that it was hard to understand him."

Later my brother was going home on a streetcar that stopped at Cincinnati Street to pick up a passenger, a taxi rolled up to the entrance of the Hotel Tulsa and a white man got out of the cab, paid his fare, picked up his bag, then turned towards the entrance of the hotel and crumpled to the sidewalk. Killed by a sniper's bullet. (One of the killings reported in several national magazines) It was thought to have been done by some of the Negros who were slipping along in the darkness on their way home from the courthouse.

Someone in the restaurant also reported that fourteen of the Negros that had been in one of the cars that were speeding around shooting up the town were now in jail. A car loaded with police officers had finally caught up with them and arrested the Negros after shooting one of them that had pointed a gun at the officers. And we learned why so many people suddenly happened to be carrying guns. All of the hardware stores and pawn shops had just been broken into and guns and ammunition taken.

Several people that we knew were in the restaurant and we told them about patrolling Boston and riding along singing harmony until the glass was shot out of the car. We weren't ready to fully appreciate their sense of humor so soon after the glass shattering ordeal. One said, "Boy, you guys must sing some terrible harmony. When it is so bad that it disturbs the neighbors until one of them takes a shot at you, it must be awful."

"Let me know before you start to sing again. I want to get as far away as possible. I thought harmony singing was supposed to be soothing and pretty, but the way you fellows sing, it must be dangerous," another one quipped.

More loud guffaws followed his sally, but we could only answer with silly, embarrassed grins. When everyone seemed to run out of giggles, one of the crowd asked, "Why don't you fellows sing some harmony? All kidding aside."

We were not about to sing for them. Not even when several others asked,

Then word was passed along in whispers, "Everyone, go to Fifteenth Street and Boulder. Pass the word and don't be late, for important plans will be explained there."

Many people were drifting out of the restaurant, so we decided to go along and see what happened at the meeting place. Driving south on Boulder we realized that several trucks and automobiles were headed for the same location, and near Fifteenth Street people had abandoned their vehicles because the streets and intersections were filled to capacity. We left the car more than a block away and began walking towards the crowded intersection. There were already three or four hundred people there and more arriving when we walked up.

A moment later a man stood up in the seat of a topless automobile (called a touring car) and spoke as loud as possible, "We have decided to go out to Second and Lewis streets and join the crowd that is meeting there. Be there in fifteen minutes. They have probably already gathered there, so don't be late."

I am certain that none of us were there in the stated time, for it took almost that long to get free from the jumbled mass of cars and people, but along with the others we hurried as fast as possible.

Arriving there it was easy to see that it was a larger crowd than the first one because the traffic jam was worse, and we could get no nearer than three blocks from the intersection. Joining several others who were walking from their vehicles, we arrived in time to hear other men standing up in cars giving instructions. One yelled to the crowd of possibly six hundred, "Men, we are going in at daylight! Nothing can stop us for there will be thousands of others going in at the same time! Meetings like this are taking place all over town and across the river in West Tulsa. Be ready at daybreak!"

All around us people were discussing what was meant by, "We are going in at daybreak."

Another man standing on top of a car interrupted the speculation with, "If any of you have more ammunition than you need, or, if what you have doesn't fit your gun, sing out, there will be somebody here that has the right caliber. Get busy and exchange shells until everybody has the right size. Then have every gun loaded and ready to shoot at daylight."

We left because we didn't need shells for a gun we didn't have. And having heard the Sheriff's explanation at the courthouse that it was all a mistake, the entire thing seemed senseless. Having no reason to doubt the Sheriff when he said that the young girl admitted that she was scared and nervous and might have made a mistake and that she was going to drop the charge against the Negro man in the morning, we believed him. And we were aware that the attempted rape story was being spread by rumors.

The police had been called while the girl was still hysterical, and the pickup order went out before the police investigation revealed the fact that it was a doubtful case of attempted rape. The suspect, Richard Rowland, was not located on the date the incident occurred, May 30, 1921. It was the following afternoon when two detectives arrested him and evidently, rumors began flying fast and furious throughout the Negro section. Agitators must have started saying that a white mob was going to hang Richard, the moment he was arrested, for only a few hours later Negro groups were courthouse bound.

The city jail was small and old and when it seemed that there might be trouble, Rowland was transferred to the new county courthouse and jail. Made of gray stone and marble imported from Italy, the county building was a much safer place for his detention, especially since the courtrooms were above the county business offices, and the jail section was at the top of the building. (Coincidentally, the marble mentioned as having been imported from Italy for the courthouse was recently sold to Tulsans as souvenirs. They paid ten times the original cost for small slabs of marble when the building was demolished. Once the pride of Tulsa, it was too small to be of benefit).[6]

The rumors about the Negro section being worked up over Rowland's arrest proved to be true. It was proven that a lot of agitation was going on over there when the groups of marching men went to demand that the Sheriff release Rowland to them. (The seventy-five we followed to the courthouse, plus the group that returned with them making a total of approximately two hundred)

As for the rumors of an impending lynching of Richard Rowland, I never saw or heard of a mob forming until after the Negros invaded the courthouse area. I have done a great amount of research and talked to many people who saw at least a part of the riot, and there simply was no lynching party there. When we followed the first group to the courthouse there was no crowd, and when the Sheriff came out to talk to the Negros, there were only around thirty of us on the lawn listening to his explanation of the situation. There may have been as many as three hundred by the time the Negros returned but it was still not a lynching party because each person that arrived began asking what was happening. Then the Sheriff came out again and explained that it was all a mistake, that no actual rape attempt had occurred.

It was natural for us to try to impress people with our special knowledge of the affair and that it was a mistake. Several times during the night we tried to explain that the killings were wrong, and that the girl had not been raped. Also, about the shot that caused the explosion to start, being accidental. But who listens to a bunch of kids at a time when most of them are fired up higher than a steam engine at a cotton gin?

Some of them ignored us, while others said, "What's the difference? They came up here hunting trouble, didn't they? So, we'll have to see that they find it."

None of them seemed to have anything in mind except, "They were asking for trouble by coming uptown with these guns and trying to take over. And when they killed those white people, they made it necessary to kill twice as many of them, so they remember what happens when they decide to shoot people."

Drinking increased steadily during the night and many people

47

became more and more fired up until the words, "We'll go get 'em soon." And "We must go kill a few to teach them a lesson," began to be heard frequently as the night wore on.

I am not positive that I can say that the situation really worried me. To some degree, it was an impersonal thing. That is, except as a spectator, I was not involved in any of the incidents. But knowing that the entire happening resulted from a mistake caused a (maybe the best description is, depressed and frustrated) saddened feeling among our group. I can remember feeling that it was all so wrong. Maybe it was a feeling for the underdog, which I have had all of my life. Whatever, it was a feeling that such killing over a mistake was very wrong, no matter how serious the mistake.

When mentioning this to the other fellows, Harry replied, "Well, we didn't start it. And we darn sure can't stop it. And it is true that the Negros came up here with these guns which touched off the trouble."

"It seems to me that they have paid a heavy price for that already. Didn't we hear that a dozen were killed and about forty wounded either at the courthouse or trying to escape from there? That is about a fourth of the entire group that marched up to the courthouse with guns," Dewey stated."

"And one more was shot and fourteen put in jail on serious charges by the police," I added.

"That is all true," Harry agreed. "But there is not a thing that we can do about it. And don't let anyone hear you talking that way, or you are apt to be hurt badly. This crowd is getting wilder by the minute and some of them are just itching for an excuse to tear into something."

This was quite true, and I have always been glad that none of us had a gun, although I am certain that none of us wanted to shoot anyone during the riot. And especially since we know how wrong the entire affair was. Yet there were others who had heard the same explanation at the courthouse and refused to believe it. Or as some were saying, "They started the trouble and we will write the finish, so they will never forget this night."

We had just decided to return to the restaurant for more coffee and rumors when two men walking by the car stopped to say, "Be ready to go at dawn."

"Be ready to go where?" we asked.

One of the men looked us over a moment before repeating, "Be ready to go where?" His voice indicated that it was incredible that there were those who could be as simple as we.

But the other man bent down to answer our query, "Be ready to go into 'nigger' town. We are going over and burn it down at daybreak. We'll teach the trouble hunters a lesson that they won't forget."

As they walked on down the street we sat in silence for a couple of minutes. None of the group offered a comment or suggestion so we continued to sit there as if waiting for someone to speak. Finally, our operator friend said, "Let's go get that coffee and pie." Everyone agreed, so we went to the restaurant and listened to the "big-talk," for a while.

We learned that the plan was for people to gather behind the long freight depot in the railroad yards which separated the Negro section from the white part of town. The mainline tracks of the MK&T, Santa Fe, and Frisco railroads, plus the storage and switching tracks made the yards very wide in that area. Everyone was to meet there at dawn.

For some time, we had been in the back part of the restaurant listening to the various rumors and different versions of the incidents that had occurred, then suddenly a new episode appeared to be developing. Becoming aware that many people were leaving the restaurant hurriedly, we watched as they quickly formed lines to pay the cashier then rush out to the street. None of us had yet voiced a question about the reason for the sudden exit of so many people before the information which caused the departure drifted back to us. Then we too joined those in line, paid the cashier, and hurried outside.

Everyone was heading in the direction of the Midland Valley Railroad, which was only about six blocks from the restaurant. It was reported that a train loaded with Negros was on the way to Tulsa from Muskogee, a distance of sixty miles to the south and east. Hundreds of people were running or walking rapidly in the direction of the passenger depot and since the distance was short we left the car parked and walked along with some of the others who apparently didn't see why it was necessary to run to the station.

Several groups of people passed us and yelled to speed it up

49

as they ran by. Quite a number of cars roared down the street carrying about all of the people that could find room to hang on the running boards. One automobile load of men drove by slow enough to shout messages to the crowds along the sidewalks. We heard them yelling while they were still about a block behind us. "Let's hurry men. The Muskogee niggers want a shootout, so we'll give it to them. Everybody hurry!"

Then as they arrived beside us they shouted, "Come on everybody! Show a little speed because we don't want that train to arrive before the greeting committee is ready to receive the guest!"

It seemed that someone was always taking charge and giving orders, and it was no different at the Midland Valley Depot. A man stepped out in front of the large crowd gathered along the tracks and on the station platform, "Now men scatter out along each side of the tracks and take cover behind the boxcars and anything else you can find to hide in or under. And some of you climb to the roof of the depot, those power and telephone poles in back will make it easy to get up there. Now everyone, get ready and when that train arrives don't let a black man get off of it and live!"

After standing around on the depot platform a little while we decided to go back uptown and get the car. There certainly wasn't anything for us to do at the depot since none of us were armed. Besides we wanted to see if it was true that all of the hardware stores and pawn shops had been broken into as we had heard. It seemed very likely because there were so many guns around. I believe that at least eighty percent of the people were armed with some type of weapon. Some of them still had price tags hanging from the trigger guards so there could be little doubt that acquirement came without purchase.

As we rode up and down the streets we found no place of business that sold firearms that had not been broken into. Every pawn shop and hardware store had a door kicked in or a display window broken out. Most of the places were already being repaired by nailing boards over the holes in the doors or across the window. Others had men guarding the opening until they could be repaired.

Harry said, "Talk about locking the barn door after the horse is gone, that old adage certainly fits this situation."

"I'll bet that a lot more than horses have been taken tonight.

Those store owners will be lucky if the guns and ammunition are the only things taken during the raids. Anytime that many people are running in and out of places that have been kicked in, you can bet your life on some of them stuffing their pockets with something," the Osage replied.

At the finish of our inspection tour of the places that had been raided someone asked, "Well, what do we do now? Are we ready to give up and go home?"

"I'm ready to go. I don't think there is anything else to see and this is probably the end of the thing," I answered,

But Harry disagreed. "I don't think this is the end. I believe that something will happen at daybreak when the crowds at the freight depot get together. I think I will wait around to see since we have been up this long. It is already four a.m. so it will only be a short wait"

Most of the others agreed and so we drove by the Midland Valley Depot to see if anything new had happened there. Nothing had, they were still waiting and since that was what we had to do we went back to the restaurant.

6. The Tulsa County Courthouse referred to was built in 1912 and demolished in 1960.

Chapter Seven

Near daybreak when the crowd in the restaurant began leaving in large numbers, we joined them because we certainly hadn't waited around all night to see what was going to happen and then not follow the action. Most of those that had left ahead of us were either walking or driving towards the chosen rendezvous location behind the freight depot in the railroad yard.

Following the crowd, we drove north on Main to First Street then turned east. A couple of blocks were as far as we could travel in that direction. A mass of cars and trucks had the street and sidewalks completely blocked at that point. Leaving the car as the others had done, we began weaving our way around and between the vehicles which had been left in such a jumbled mess.

Several hundred others must have been doing the same thing for the glow from pipes, cigarettes, and cigars could be seen bobbing along in the darkness as those ahead of us worked their way towards Elgin Avenue. We were still two blocks from there when I noticed the old store buildings which we were passing. Until recent years, this section had been a part of Tulsa's main business district.

My memory flashed back to three years before when a couple of those old buildings played a part in Tulsa's share of the worldwide tragedy of the 1918 Spanish Influenza epidemic. It has been estimated at least ten million people died during the fall months of that year. Since there was no spot on earth not touched by the malignant epidemic, history has not recorded anything that has come close to scourging the earth with such deadly results.

Tulsa found itself in the middle of a catastrophe for which it was less prepared than other cities of comparable size. Having grown from approximately eighteen thousand people to a population of sixty-five thousand within a short interval of eight years, it had been built so fast that it had not been able to keep pace in the facilities necessary to serve its citizens. There was almost no progress at all in such things as nurses, doctors, and hospitalization facilities that might be needed in case of an emergency.

Suddenly Tulsa was caught with its britches at half-mast. Silent and deadly, the pernicious pestilence began its attack. People became ill while walking down the street or while sitting in a restaurant. One moment they were walking along and the next their bodies crumpled to the sidewalk, or slipped off a stool into the floor deathly ill.

An emergency hospital was set up in one of the old storage buildings. Some of the schools and churches were filled with victims of the flu and still, there was not enough space available. Many hundreds had to fight through the ordeal in their homes. At one period there were more than three thousand people down with the disease. Quite a percentage of the population when one considers that during the epidemic a total of approximately nine thousand of the sixty-five thousand had the flu and up to fifteen people died each day.

The city officials and health authorities banned all gatherings of any sort. People were even advised not to shake hands with friends, Then it was decided that all persons not engaged in a necessary service should be put in quarantine. Hustling girls, especially, were considered as spreaders of the disease so the authorities began raiding the district which everyone said didn't exist. Pimps, gamblers, bootleggers, and prostitutes were brought in by the dozens. Two of the old warehouse buildings that we were now passing on our way to the rendezvous, were taken over and turned into places of confinement for the city's undesirables which were to be held in quarantine.

I was sixteen-years-old when the flu epidemic spread affliction, misery, and death over the earth. When school closed for the summer I went to work for the telephone company as a lineman's helper. Because Tulsa was in the middle of such frenzied, booming activity every company was seeking help and any person sixteen years of age or over could go to work immediately. I worked with the lineman until the fall term was ready to start, then quit to enroll for the next nine months of school.

At the time, many Tulsans were becoming ill with what the doctors diagnosed as the grippe. Within two weeks, it had grown to epidemic intensity and the news reports stated that it was worldwide. Thousands of cases were reported from the army camps where the American soldiers were being trained for action in World War I.

Finally, it was discovered to be a new type of influenza and it was not only spreading rapidly, but people began dying faster than burial crews could dig graves. It was then that the Tulsa authorities realized that drastic action had to be taken. Ordinances were passed banning gatherings, the quarantine raids began, and schools were closed for the duration of the emergency.

The telephone company crew foreman contacted me and asked if I could come back to work as long as the school had to be kept closed. He said that so many workers were off because of illness that they were simply swamped with work. I agreed to return for the duration of the emergency.

One of the first assignments given to the lineman whom I worked with all summer was the installing of telephones in the two buildings that were being used to confine those people gathered up in the quarantine raids. Two linemen were sent to do the job, but I was the only helper. One of them was needed to make the necessary wire splices for the hook-up on the outside cable, while the other would run the wiring inside the building and installed the phones.

After rigging up the platform we pulled it up to the lineman above us and he hooked it onto the cable near the pole. The lineman on the ground gathered up rolls of wire and his tools and went in the back door of one building while I pulled the tools up to the man on the platform by hand rope.

After sending up all of the equipment needed to the man on the platform, I was free to relax until he called for something else. Then I happened to glance into the window nearest to me and discovered that there were people inside. I also discovered that they were all women. Some seemed to be very little older than me, and really pretty.

Then, they discovered me standing in the alley staring into the window. Possibly because they were bored from having been cooped up in the building for a day or two, they saw a chance to have some fun with a gawky kid. One of them walked over to the window, raised her foot to the windowsill, then threw open her robe to expose a leg up to her panties. And at the same time asked, "How would you like to come here and feel my muscle?"

Had I known in advance what to expect, it is doubtful that I could have kept from turning my head away. Hearing laughter from several of them I stole a quick glance in the direction then hastily lowered my eyes and again turned my head. This really turned the laughter on. It also brought more of them to the windows until even those on the second floor were filled with girls of every type.

Finding someone so shy he couldn't look at partly nude bodies without blushing and turning away made their day. Others began showing their legs and breasts and the things they said were just as embarrassing as what they did. If I could have stood there and taken a good look, or had I turned my back and not glanced at them again, they would have lost interest in a hurry.

But as a young kid freshly moved to the big "wicked city," I did neither. Less than a year away from a little country town where seeing a woman's knee was a daring experience, I simply couldn't cope with what was happening. And yet, I couldn't ignore it completely either. I kept sneaking quick glances and trying to act nonchalant at the same time. Their laughter was almost hysterical as they tried to top others' performances while observing my reactions. In the idiom of today, they did their thing, and I blushed.

Finally, there was nothing left to do except to get down to the "nitty-gritty" and that they did by leaving nothing to the imagination. Several of them took off whatever they were wearing under their robes and stood there in their birthday clothes. Then in case they hadn't already knocked me deaf and dumb, they dotted the I's and crossed the T's by telling me that they wanted me to decide which I preferred. Three of them lined up in front of the window as one asked, "Which would you rather spend the night with, a blonde, brunette, or redhead?"

If the lineman up on the platform hadn't spoken up at that moment I am certain that I would have quit and gone home. Up near the wall and off to the side, he could hear but couldn't see them.

"Why don't you come over to this other window so I can see what you are showing too?" he asked.

One of them replied, "Hell no. You would enjoy it too much."

Then he stated, "Well that kid is not enjoying it very much. He is only sixteen and hasn't seen much of that stuff."

"That may have been true a little while ago, but now he has seen more than any other kid in town," one of them replied.

My mind jumped back to what was happening then and there as we reached Elgin Avenue and one of the fellows said, "Look at the mass of automobiles and trucks all headed toward the intersection from the west, south, and east. Did you ever see such a traffic jam?"

"I didn't know that there were that many vehicles in Tulsa. There must be one hell of a mob of people down in the railroad yards." Harry replied.

Turning north on Elgin, we continued walking around cars until we were near the office portion of the freight depot a half block north of First Street. The bumper-to-bumper jam of automobiles stopped there. No one had been brave enough to come in from the north because the Negro section was just across the railroad yards.

Continuing to wend our way around the cars we crossed the street to the south side of the long freight building. Switching tracks ran alongside the leading platforms on either side for the entire length of the building. There was room on the south side of the building to shelter a huge crowd and judging by the glowing red dots that flickered brighter as people puffed on their smokes, Harry had been right when he said, "There must be one hell of a mob of people in the railroad yards."

Frankfort, the first street to the east of Elgin, was not a through street. It stopped on either side of the tracks so the freight depot might have been more than a block long. Deciding to walk to the eastern end of the building we were forced to step out a considerable distance from it because the huge mass of people was gathered in its shelter from one end to the other.

Not only did the glowing dots of burning tobacco extend the entire length of the building, they could be seen on down the tracks from behind dark objects which were apparently boxcars on the sidings. It seemed that people were behind every object that was large enough to shield them from any snipers that might possibly be waiting for enough light to find a target.

Mingling with those who were already gathered at the east end of the building, we learned that some of them had just left the Midland Valley Railroad where they had waited most of the night for the train which was supposed to arrive from Muskogee loaded with Negros coming to help those in Tulsa. The train did not arrive. Seemed to be just another rumor.

It was learned later, however, that a number of cars and trucks that were loaded with all of the people that they could carry did drive down the highway toward Muskogee and set up roadblocks to stop any Negros that might try to come to Tulsa by automobile. This proved to be not a rumor because several vehicles loaded with Negros were stopped at the roadblocks, disarmed, and the keys to their vehicles taken from them and thrown out in a pasture in the darkness while the Negros were sent running back toward Muskogee as fast as their feet could carry them.

As daylight approached a little nearer, several long dark objects which I now know to be stacks of oilwell pipe, could be seen along the north side of the railroad tracks. Red embers of burning tobacco indicated that large numbers of people were using the long rows of metal pipe as sheltering barriers. Because Frankfort Street dead-ended at the tracks, the pile of oil well pipe which was just to the north of the right-of-way was strung out on across where the street would have crossed the tracks. The glowing embers of burning tobacco moved up and down the stacks of pipe as people climbed to the top and peeped over toward the Negro section which was still bathed in the murky darkness of the early morning.

Archer is the first street north and runs parallel with the tracks and was named for a well-known pioneer family. The old street was lined with tired dilapidated buildings and shacks that were left over from the days when Tulsa was a village. The oil strike started a building boom south of the tracks and when Tulsa continued to sweep in that direction, the Negro section expanded into the old buildings along Archer Street.

When the tragic event about which this writer is narrating occurred, all of the businesses on Archer from Detroit Street east, were owned or operated by Negros. Consisting of small cafes, barbershops, poolhalls, tailor shops, and other small businesses, Archer Street was not in the main business section of the Negro district. The few old buildings with two or three stories usually had a cheap hotel or some dilapidated apartments above the dull appearing little business below. It was a tired droopy old street in a new city.

The MK&T Railroad tracks ran through the same switching yards where the crowd was now gathered but had separate facilities otherwise. The Santa Fe and Frisco railroads used the main passenger depot which was down the tracks about three blocks west of the building we were behind.

We were not aware that fateful morning that another crowd of comparable size was gathered at that passenger depot. And yet another group which was somewhat smaller was waiting for daylight at the MK&T depot, three blocks north of the Santa Fe-Frisco passenger depot.

While standing at the east end of the freight building and waiting for daybreak to edge a little closer, people stood in small groups, or maybe larger clusters, and chatted. Whether it was an individual or a group of people, all were surrounded by a sea of faces that were as yet not entirely recognizable if more than arm's length away. Now and then, one or two of these at the end of the building stepped out from its shelter to stand and stare for a moment toward the Negro section to the north. It was still murky dark in that area.

It seemed that the light of dawn had just started sweeping away some of the shadowy darkness when a young man in a white shirt stepped from behind the building to gaze toward the north for a moment, then went down with a gasp. Two men jumped out, grabbed his feet, and drug him back to the shelter of the building. They pulled him to within five feet of where I was standing before they started to examine his condition. A mass of people surged forward and engulfed us as most of those who were nearby crowded in to see what was happening. I was shoved almost on top of the two men who were trying to help the young man that had been shot.

Someone turned the rays of a flashlight on the victim who was lying on his back. One of the men tore open the front of his shirt and in the center of his solar plexus area was a spot about the size of the end of a cigarette which turned a reddish blue color. A small amount of blood oozed from the hole and formed a little pool in the pit of his stomach.

His eyes were rolling toward the top of his head and although not more than half a dozen drops of blood had beaded up from the small blue-rimmed spot in his stomach, it came gushing from his mouth with each gasp. Only a few moments after the men began their examination, the flow of blood slowed, and the gulping and gasping ceased and one of the men ran his hand under the body of the young man. When he withdrew his hand, it was covered with so much blood that it dripped to the ground and someone yelled, "Get an ambulance!"

Wiping his hand on a handkerchief as he stood up the man said, "It's too late for him, he is dead."

Suddenly I was hot and perspiring all over. I wanted out of there in a hurry. It was difficult to breathe with the mass of people squeezing in tighter and tighter as everyone tried to get a look at the dead body. Nearly overwhelmed by giddiness, I began struggling to get out of the crowding, shoving, mob of onlookers. Covered with cold sweat, I finally broke out of the crowd and walked over to some boxcars standing on a siding behind the depot and my friends followed to see what was wrong with me.

I explained about becoming very ill as the crowd packed in tight and seemed to breathe in all of the air leaving me cold, sweating, and struggling to get my breath.

Harry replied, "You probably became ill because you stared too intently at the young man as he died. Some people are affected in this manner."

Whatever the cause, I leaned against one of the boxcars and gave up the coffee and waffle I had eaten earlier. I felt some better but was still ready to call off my part of watching whatever was going to happen at daybreak and go home. So, I explained to the others how I felt and admitted, "It may be as Harry said, I watched so closely as his eyes rolled over toward the top of his head and blood gushed from his mouth, that it simply got to me, I guess." I went on to explain about being ready to go home because I still felt bad.

While walking back toward Elgin Avenue they began discussing the details of the young man's death. "I seem to remember that he was smoking a cigarette when he stepped from behind the building," our Osage friend said.

The operator agreed, "That's true. He took a drag from it a moment before he went down."

Harry added, "It was probably the white shirt and the ciga-rette combined that made him a good target for the sniper with a high-powered rifle. Everyone agreed that it was a high-powered rifle because the bullet passed completely through his body.

Arriving back at Elgin Avenue where we had first joined the crowd behind the building, I had not had time to remind the oth-ers that I was going home before a Franklin automobile stopped when its headlights outlined the crowd gathered on the south side of the freight depot.

There were a couple of hundred people within hearing dis-tance of the voice that yelled from the Franklin, "What the hell are you waitin' on? Let's go get 'em!"

How the driver had managed to get past the jammed intersec-tion was a mystery for not only the streets were impassable, even the sidewalks were blocked by automobiles for quite a distance. There were five men in the Franklin, which must have been driven down the railroad tracks a couple of blocks before reaching Elgin Street.

The dawning of a new day seemed to approach slowly as if reluctant to chase away the darkness which would be a signal for action by the huge mob that was waiting impatiently for daylight. Just enough light had arrived to create a silhouette of the automo-bile and identify it as a Franklin and the small light inside the car made it possible to count, but not recognize the men. Again, one of them shouted, "Well, we asked what are you waiting for? Come on let's go get the job done!" He drank from a bottle and passed it on.

Someone in the crowd near the building answered, "We are waiting for a little daylight, then we are going in."

From the Franklin, a voice replied, "That's a lot of bullshit. You're a bunch of yellow bellies. So, stay here where it's safe and we'll do the job for you."

With that the automobile roared off north toward Archer Street then turned east, headed for the main part of the Negro district.

Ten or fifteen seconds later dozens of shots from pistols, rifles, and shotguns, were heard coming from that direction.

It had been a long time coming but that fusillade triggered the action. With wild frenzied shouts, men began pouring from behind the freight depot and the long strings of boxcars and evidently from behind the piles of oilwell casing which was at the other end and on the north side of the building. From every place of shelter up and down the tracks came screaming, shouting men to join in the rush toward the Negro section. Mingled with the shouting were a few rebel-yells and Indian gobblings as the great wave of humanity rushed forward totally absorbed in thoughts of destruction.

The shooting and the yelling as the mob broke from behind the sheltering barriers evidently touched off action by the other mob of people who we didn't know had gathered at the passenger depot. Suddenly hundreds of people came running down the tracks from that direction. More yelling and screaming with flashes of gunfire in the air told of other hundreds hurrying east on Archer Street. Then the headlights of many cars were seen going east on the streets parallel and to the north of Archer. An indication that more hundreds of people had been waiting in their automobiles, ready to head east.

Later it was learned that yet another crowd of a few hundred had been gathering at the MK&T (Katy) depot about five blocks north and west of our location. In a matter of minutes, the great masses of people came together in the outer edges of the southwestern section of the Negro district and began spreading out and destroying everything as they went.

The size of the total mob could never be anything more than a guess. It was estimated by most people to have been between fifteen and twenty thousand. My guess, as good as any, because I saw great masses of frenzied rioters as well as fragments of the mob during sixteen or seventeen hours of observation throughout the entire area, has always been that approximately fifteen thousand people were in the invasion. I believe that up to four-fifths of the mob were actually involved in the rioting and the others were sightseers watching the spectacle. Since we were spectators and not involved in destroying anything we had much more time to observe what was happening than those who were always rushing on to the next object they were bent on exterminating. I remember seeing many people who had cameras and were photographing everything. Some of them I saw a number of times at different places, always taking pictures.

The feeling of weakness and nausea which had led to my decision to go home was forgotten when the wild screaming mob sprang into action and went scurrying by us so fast that in a moment or two we were left almost alone. Only a few people remembered their automobiles were parked nearby. The rest simply ran off to the north leaving their abandoned cars blocking the street or sidewalk.

Our driver said, "Come on, let's get the car." And we joined the few others who were trying to push and shove enough of the abandoned vehicles to free their own from the jammed-up mass. It probably took us ten or more minutes to shove enough cars back and forth to maneuver free of the tangle at the place we had parked. Every so often we stopped for a moment to listen when it seemed that the gunfire became heavier. Then, by the time we climbed in the car and began backing and turning to drive down the narrow path we had opened up, a reddish glow began lighting up the darkness which hovered over the area. The first buildings that the mob had reached on Archer, were on fire.

Chapter Eight

Crossing the tracks at Cincinnati we turned east on Archer Street and saw many people coming from the direction of the business district who were headed toward the Negro section. They couldn't have been a part of the crowd that had waited at the depot to attack at daybreak. Very few of them seemed to be armed, indicating that they were more apt to be "lookers, than doers."

Flames were consuming several of the old buildings on Archer and as we reached the spot where the Negro section began it was apparent that all of them were on fire. Also, the houses north of Archer on Detroit and Elgin streets were breaking out in flames proving that the mob was bent on the total obliteration of everything destructible.

By the time we arrived at Elgin Avenue enough light from the fires and early dawn made it possible to identify things up to a distance of around three hundred feet. Several people were gathered around an automobile out in the middle of Archer, near Frankfort Street. We realized as we approached, that it evidently was the Franklyn that had led the dash toward the Negro section which caused the pent-up emotions of the mob to explode into action.

People who were hurrying by stopped to look briefly into the Franklin, then dashed on to the north or east to overtake the main body of rioters. As we stopped, stragglers continued to hesitate a moment at the green car, then dash on toward the action. We joined them to examine the Franklin. It was riddled with bullet holes, and shotgun pellets had peppered the car making little dents in the body and knocking paint off the doors. There wasn't a piece of glass as large as my hand left in the windows or doors of the Franklin.

Then we saw why people hurried on after a brief look into the car. There wasn't a thing that could be done for the five men inside. They were slumped in a bloody mess on top of each other or crumpled on the floor. It was not a sight to stand and stare at for long, just masses of torn and bloody, gray flesh. The five bodies were beyond the help of man. They would not mind waiting to be disposed of, so we hurried back to the car and drove away.

Smoke and flames came from all of the old shacks and the few brick buildings on Archer and all of the houses as far as we could see up Detroit and Elgin, and even past Frankfort were burning as we hurried away from the Franklin and its burden of horror. And yet it had been no more than fifteen minutes since we left the freight depot after the rioters had gone rampaging into the Negro district.

It was not yet completely daylight, but fire from all of the burning buildings and houses was casting a reddish hue against the darker background of early dawn when Harry suggested that we drive over and climb to the top of Standpipe Hill and see how much of the Negro section was burning.

Leaving the car at the foot of the hill on Cincinnati Street, we walked over and began climbing the steep hill. The weeds at the top were shoulder high and as we walked through them toward the east side, we approached with caution knowing that there was a deep hole on the eastern rim of the hill. It was a sheer drop-off of a couple of hundred feet into the old abandoned brick plant pit.

The tall weeds grew up to the edge of the cliff and we arrived to discover that we were not the only ones with the idea of seeing the riot from the hilltop. At least twenty people were already there crouched in the weeds. As we came near some of them yelled for us to hit the ground quickly. Needing no second warning we dropped down in the weeds alongside the others gathered along the top of the steep cliff.

The top of the hill was lighter than the valley below and the morning light highlighted a silhouette of anyone standing by the cliff. A moment before we arrived, a sniper in the valley took a shot at some of those who were standing up near the pit. Crouching low in the shorter weeds and grass that lined the very edge of the pit, we watched the fires creep forward as the rioters put a match to everything they came upon that would burn.

It was still murky dark below and not much of anything could be seen except the shadowy bulk of the houses until the fires burned bright enough to light up the immediate area and expose the rioters as they ran from house to house, committing arson. It was eerie because up ahead of the fires there was only murkiness, then another fire flickered to life seemingly without cause as no members of the mob were visible except these back near the houses that were already burning.

A few minutes later it became light enough to see people running back and forth across the streets and from house to house like little ants. The sun was beginning to peep over the horizon when I noticed a group of people kneeling or crouching in the weeds about forty feet from where we were sitting.

They were gathered around a man that I had seen in the business section several times within the last few days. He was dressed in the same manner as before, white breeches that laced from the ankles to his knees, with leggings, or "putts" covering the calf of each leg. His shirt was white also, and on his head was a white pith helmet of the sort shown in motion pictures of men on safaris in Africa.

Each time that I had seen him in the downtown district, he had been standing beside a white Stutz Bearcat automobile which was covered with signs painted in black letters. I do not remember the exact wording of the signs, but they were such things as," Bombay-To Mandalay — Barnes-To Port Said — Capetown-To Singapore," and dozens of others.

As he stood beside the white Stutz, he made a pitch to sell picture postcards of himself standing beside a dead lion or holding a rifle in his hand as he rode on the back of an elephant. In some of the other pictures, he was standing beside a beautiful pagoda. He told people who stopped to listen that he was a world traveler and sold the postcards to finance his trips around the world.

As he sat in the woods explaining to those gathered around him about the heavy hunting rifle he held in his hand, I crawled over to get a look at the rifle with the odd peep-sight which he demonstrated by pushing it up and down.

The man who called himself, "Captain — " something, I have forgotten the last name but believe it was, Wonder — or Wander — something, lifted up the strange-looking peep-sight on the rifle with which he claimed to have killed tigers, elephants, and lions and said, "I can kill anything I hit at a distance of four hundred yards."[7]

It had grown light enough to permit a view of several feet down into the darkened old abandoned hole in the side of the hill. Pointing to the north rim where a man was just emerging from the shadows as he climbed slowly toward the top of the pit, the "Traveling Man," said, "I could easily knock that man off the wall from here if I wanted to, but I'll just give him a good scare. Wait until he reaches the top and I'll put a bullet right at his feet, then watch him hop."

I continued to watch the man climbing up the eroded clay bank. He was just below the curving north rim of the pit. It didn't seem possible that anyone could climb out of that deep hole along the steep, crumbly wall of the old cliff. Then I noticed a couple of other climbers as they came out of the murky shadows just below the first man.

The man in the African safari garb spoke again as the first man reached the top. "Now I'll show you how to make him scoot out of there. I'll dig some dirt right by his feet the moment he stands up on top." With that, he pumped a shell into the rifle barrel and adjusted the sight to his satisfaction.

Looking at the face of the precipitous clay bank I decided that anyone that climbed out of the old pit would have to be very strong and athletic. At that moment the first man reached the top and stood up. Then true to his promise, Captain— whatever his name, slammed a couple of bullets into the dirt beside him, and from the instant reaction, they must have been close. He leaped aside, then dove into the nearby weeds. It seemed a wonder that the excitement and fear from the shots hadn't caused one of the others to fall.

I crawled back where my friends were and told them that I thought it was rather silly shooting off that rifle just to make people jump.

"He is showing off for what he considers to be a bunch of 'hicks' in a country town," Harry said, then added, "That is not a great shooting exhibition. Anyone who can shoot at all can do that well with a good rifle."

He watched to see if the self-professed "big game hunter and world traveler," was going to show off his prowess by shooting to scare any more of the Negros climbing on the wall, but he didn't shoot again. He became so engrossed in explaining about the rifle to what he must have realized was an admiring audience of eight or ten people, that he forgot about the Negros who by that time had increased to about four or five climbing up out of the shadows.

Someone suggested that we leave for we had seen about all that we could see from the hilltop. We crawled back into the tall weeds before standing up, for we were aware that it had turned to daylight while we were up there and any sniper that might shoot at us would not be playing games as had the "Traveling Man."

Making certain that we were well concealed in the woods we stood and gazed down on a large part of the Negro section. The sun had chased the shadows from almost the entire scene below during the approximately forty-five minutes that we had been on the hill. After staring into the valley a few minutes one of the fellows said, "I have never seen anything like it. Isn't that something?"

The movie operator answered, "It's something all right. And you will probably never see anything like it again in your life."

7. There was a Captain Walter Wanderwell who was an adventurer touring the world about this time and documenting his exploits. No proof he is the same man mentioned here, but possibly the man in question.

Chapter Nine

Smoke was drifting high into the calm morning air beginning at Archer Street and extending northward block after block into the Negro section. At the same time, the fire and smoke continued moving to the east, step by step as the rows of houses on each side of the streets were ignited. Flames sprang up around the edge of the Negro business district to the east also as the arsonists moved in relentlessly from every direction.

The most remarkable thing was the change that had occurred between the time of our arrival and when we were ready to depart. When arriving, the only means of measuring the progress of the rioters was the glow of new fires as the houses burst into flames of destruction. When leaving, the sun had climbed high enough in the sky to change from a giant red ball into a great mass of blinding brightness and the smoke of burning houses and buildings was a better indication of the mob's progress than the flames.

There was not a single structure behind the rioters that was not burning. The first of the buildings along Archer Street that were set afire was now beginning to crumble and even the smoke was dying out around some of the buildings. Black smoke, brown, gray, and white smoke floated skyward from all of the areas where the mob had been. The sound of rifle fire seemed to be coming from the direction of the Negro business district, which suggested the reason why only the outer edges of that section had been put to the torch.

When leaving the hill, a decision was made to drive over to the streets where the houses were being set afire and get a close-up look at what was happening. We drove south on Cincinnati to the first cross street and turned east. At Elgin Avenue a large crowd was gathered in the intersection a block south of us, hesitating only a moment to look the situation over, we headed there to see what was happening. All of the houses were burning, and the heat was fierce as we rolled up to the intersection which was blocked by about seventy-five Negros being guarded by four or five white men. The mob had gone to make war on more houses leaving the few guards to handle the action at the rear.

One of the white men walked over to us as we rolled to a stop and asked, "Why don't you fellows take these people to the police station? You can follow along behind them in your car."

Protesting that we were not involved in the riot and were following the crowd only to see what happened, Harry informed the guard that we didn't even have a gun.

"You don't need a gun for this job," the man insisted. "These people will not try to escape because they know that the safest place for them is at the police station away from flying bullets."

"Why don't you just leave them here?" I asked. "There is certainly nothing that they can do here that will cause any harm."

"If they are left here to run loose, some of them will be shot. They must be taken in for their own protection," the man explained.

After a moment of discussion, we told the men guarding the group, "All right we'll take them to the station but if any of them decide to run, we won't be able to stop them for we are not armed."

"They won't run because they know that the best place for them is in a crowd guarded by white men," the same spokesman stated.

One of the other men stepped forward and handed a twenty-two rifle to Harry as he said, "Here take this, I don't need it." Then pulled a revolver from under his belt.

After telling the Negros to head south down Elgin Avenue, the former guards headed north toward where new columns of smoke indicated that the mob was still busy destroying property and we drove off following the Negros heading south. As they plodded down the street between the rows of burning houses, the heat from the fires and the sun was almost suffocating. Most of the clothing worn by the Negros was soaked by perspiration and we were beginning to drip moisture from our chins like leaky faucets.

Feeling uncomfortable didn't adequately describe how those poor Negros must have felt as they trudged slowly down Elgin toward Archer Street. I was simply miserable from the heat and that had to be the least of their worries as they struggled along, some of them so old that they were almost feeble and others so young that walking that distance was a task.

The city jail, police station, and the municipal courtroom were located a half-block west of Main, on Second Street. It had taken approximately twenty minutes to travel eight blocks from where the Negros had been rounded up near the edge of their district where the mob began the raid.

While riding back toward the rioting area, Harry started examining the rifle. After a moment he laughed and shook his head over his discovery, "It is a good thing that we didn't need this. There is not a single shell in it, and I'll bet my hat that it wouldn't shoot if we had shells. It is old and worn out, probably hasn't been shot in years."

The same thought crossed my mind as Dewey said, "That is the kind of rifle that might have been in one of those pawn shops that were broken into last night."

Great billows of black smoke were visible a few blocks to the east as we drove back to the Negro section. It indicated that the rioters had made some progress into the business district. Burning houses did not create that much black smoke. It was caused by inflammable material stored in warehouses and other places of business.

The houses that were burning to the north and northeast sent up clouds of dirty gray colored smoke and occasionally a few puffs of short-lived brown or black smoke which was caused when something of an extra inflammable nature happened to be in a house. Mainly the house fires created brownish-gray clouds of vapor which turned white as they began dying out. The heavy black smoke billowed up from the Greenwood area north of Archer Street, the main business district of the Negro section.

A few blocks beyond where we began the trip to the station with the Negros, there was a second bunch of them in the street. Again, we were asked to take them into the station. And again, we protested that we were not a part of the rioters, but spectators, only. But as before, we allowed some men to persuade us to go with the group of about forty Negros to prevent some of the "Trigger Happy Crowd" from shooting them.

There were no real young or old people in the second group, so even though the trip was several blocks longer, it was made in about the same length of time. At the station, they told us not to bring anymore there because they were overflowing with Negro refugees. We were informed that even the halls and the courtroom where the morning session of Municipal Court had been canceled, were filled to capacity. We were instructed to pass the word along that any other refugees should be taken to the Convention Hall.

On our way back to the burning district from our second trip to the police station, our driver said, "I am not going to herd any more people to wherever they are being sent. Look at that gauge. Driving along that slow behind people who are walking heats the car up too much."

I glanced at the gauge and the needle was definitely pointing to the danger zone. "I don't blame that gauge for screaming danger. It is hot enough to roast a pig. Why don't we keep away from between the rows of burning houses where the heat climbs so high?" I asked.

"If we drove up to near the head of the mob where the leaders are it wouldn't be so hot. The fires haven't had time to heat up things there, and we can also see what happens as they come to buildings and houses not yet set on fire," Harry suggested.

Our driver turned at the next corner but had driven less than a block when a couple of men stepped out in front of us and held up their hands for us to stop. As we complied one of the men pointed to a couple of Negros that were on the ground near the curb and informed us, "These men are severely wounded. One of them is in real bad shape. He has been shot in both legs and has lost a lot of blood. The other one has been shot in the shoulder and they both need medical attention in a hurry. How about driving them to a hospital?"

The man that had been shot in the shoulder was holding an old coat to the wound as he sat on the ground and rocked back and forth. The other one was stretched out on the ground moaning in pain as he grasped a leg with one hand and clutched a handful of grass with the other.

The car belonged to the Indian, so he had to make the decision. Finally making up his mind, he turned off the motor, took the keys, climbed out and walked to the back of his car, and opened the trunk. After tumbling things around for a moment, he pulled out an oiled raincoat or slicker and said, "This is all I have to keep the blood from getting on the upholstery. Maybe we can wrap it around the feet and legs of the one that has been shot there and the other one can hold the coat against the wound tight enough to keep from bleeding on the seat."

With that, we loaded the two Negros in the back seat and three members of our group climbed in the front. Then, with two of us riding on the front fenders, we headed for the nearest hospital where I am sorry to say we had some trouble because they refused to take the Negros. They said that the hospital was so full that they could not take one more person.

We thought that it was because the men were Negros and said so. Still, they refused, saying that they simply had no room for anyone. We held a short conference then told those who were in charge at the hospital that we were going to leave the men at their door, and that it was up to them whether they let the men bleed to death or not.

Doing just that, we went to the car and drove away. We were positive that they would not let the men die by their door, and it was a way of forcing them to care for the Negros. It is quite possible that we were wrong about the men being turned down because they were black. We learned later that the hospitals were filled to capacity and that many Negros were treated in them. However, most of the Negros who were wounded were taken to the National Guard Armory which was turned into an emergency hospital.

Returning to the automobile, we discovered that the back seat would have to be cleaned before it could be used. When the Osage saw the blood on the seat cushions, and the floor, he used some choice words then headed for the nearest gasoline station. After using the water hose to wash off the cushion and floor and borrowing some wiping rags to dry the upholstery as much as possible, we thanked the station attendant, bought five gallons of gasoline, and drove away with two of us riding on the front fender until the sun dried the back seat.

Smoke was spiraling up much farther north and east than before as we returned toward where the rioters continued their destruction. From the slowly moving smoke pattern, it was evident that the mob was spreading their devastation in the shape of a fan with Detroit as the western, and Archer Street as the southern edge of the holocaust.

To avoid the heat from driving between the rows of burning houses we drove on Cincinnati, a block west of the fires. Then just before reaching the dead-end streets at the foot of Standpipe Hill, we turned east hoping to come in close to the leading groups of rioters and avoid the worst of the heat. Believing that the mob's leaders were somewhere to the east of the hill, we headed in that direction.

Suddenly we were surprised to come upon some National Guardsmen standing in the street. They simply stood there watching the burning and the people streaming past them. Our driver rolled the car up near one of the guardmens before stopping and since I was sitting on a fender on that side of the automobile, I asked what they were doing there.

"Hell, I don't know," he replied. "We were called for emergency duty then rushed out here and spread out along a line about a mile in length. On the way here, we were informed that we would be lined up ahead of the mob and when the rioters approached, we were to stop them."

"How many guards did they call out?" I asked.

"The call was for all guardsmen to report to the armory, but they could only contact sixty-five of us on such short notice."

"How did they expect sixty-five guards to stop thousands of rioting people?" Dewey asked from the other fender.

"God only knows, I sure don't. When they drove along here on a truck and dropped five or six off at each intersection people were already running past us by the hundreds. The lieutenant in command jumped from the truck and tried to stop them by yelling 'Halt! Stop!' But even while he was yelling, several hundred more rushed by just like we weren't here."

"What did the officer do then?" Harry asked from the automobile when the guardsmen had finished his explanation.

"He told us to stand by while he went to call for reinforcements. That was about half an hour ago and I'll bet that ten thousand people have gone through our line since then."

Sixty-five men trying to stop a mob of twenty thousand people who were running amuck was about as hopeless as trying to dip Lake Erie dry with a spoon. What a tragic situation to be caught in.

A feeling of weak and deficient uselessness must have been the lot of the sixty-five National Guardsmen as they stood with fixed bayonets on their rifles while watching a rioting mob of several thousand people burn everything in sight and kill anyone that resisted. Not being able to do a thing about it had to be a humiliating experience. Had it not been such a horrible situation, it would have been ludicrous.

Remembering what the large, rough voiced man said to the ambulance driver as he shoved the rifle into his stomach, I knew that one thrust at a rioter with a bayonet and there would be a bunch of dead guardsmen, and the rioting would continue as if they had not died. Nothing except a much stronger force could stop the riot, and such a force was not available.

As we left the frustrated guardsmen, great clouds of smoke hung over the entire area that was visible to the south and east of the hill. Everything was burning or had already been turned to ashes. The holocaust was created because of man's hatred of men of another color.

When the gauge again indicated that the automobile was dangerously hot the Indian stopped to let it cool down. All of us climbed out to stretch and look around and after a moment or two Dewey said, "This is the most senseless thing I ever saw in my life."

"It's not just senseless, it's stupid," Harry replied. "Makes me believe that everything the Negros told us on the way to the hospital was true."

"What did they say?" I asked Harry.

He seemed puzzled for a moment then, "That's right, two of you were riding on the fenders at the time and didn't hear them. They told us that they had not heard about the trouble last night. They went to bed early because they had to start for work at dawn, they had quite a distance to travel.

"They stated that they finished breakfast at about six a.m. then heard something that sounded like gunshots. Going to a window they raised the shade and saw that several houses were burning to the south of them. Before they had time to discuss the situation, several men kicked in the door, pointed guns at them, then grabbed and slammed them against the wall and told them not to move or even breathe hard or they would be shot."

When Harry hesitated as if trying to remember what else the Negros had said, our Osage friend added, "They also informed us that one man stood guard with a rifle pointed at them while the others searched the house. And while the others were searching, their guard kept telling them that if anyone else was found hiding in the house it would mean they were guilty and all of them would be shot.

"One of the searchers found what the older Negros described as an old twenty-two rifle on a closet. He smelled of the barrel and said, 'This rifle has been fired recently,' Then while they were trying to explain about hunting rabbits on Sunday and failed to clean the rifle, the man guarding them raised his rifle and shot the older Negro in the shoulder."

The movie projectionist added, "It is probably a good thing that the young Negro panicked and ran when his father was shot or the shotgun blast that he took in the legs as he reached the porch, might have been in his belly.

"They also said that if it had not been for some of the other men in the search party, both of them would have been killed. A couple of them grabbed the man who shot the father, while the others wrestled with the one that had the shotgun to prevent him from firing a second shot into the young Negro."

Harry continued, "They told us that the only way the others could get the two that wanted to keep shooting to calm down was by telling them, 'Look, let's leave them alive to spread the word about what happens to niggers that hunt trouble. We'll teach them a lesson that they won't forget by leaving them shot up and setting fire to their damn house.' The older Negro reported that the man dragged his son off the porch onto the lawn, set fire to the house, and left."

It was a common practice during the riot to search a house for weapons and shoot any Negro man if a gun was found. Sometimes the shots were fatal. Of course, very few Negros were found in the houses before they were set on fire. The people had grabbed their children and what few possessions they could carry and fled ahead of the mob.

Smoke billowing from the fires that engulfed the African American section of Tulsa, Okla., known as the Greenwood District, May 31 and June 1, 1921.

The rampaging mobs laid waste to one of the most successful African American communities in the United States. So vibrant and successful that it was known as Black Wall Street.

Following World War I, the Greenwood District of Tulsa was considered one of the most affluent African American communities in the United States. However, the Tulsa Race Massacre of 1921 left it a pile of rubble and ash.

The Tulsa Race Massacre of 1921 destroyed more than 1,200 homes and businesses, left several hundred people dead and erased years of Black success.

This photo of the author, William C. "Choc" Phillips, was taken in 1919, two years prior to the 1921 Tulsa Race Massacre. *Family Archives*

Oklahoma National Guardsmen marching African Americans through the streets of Tulsa for internment during the 1921 Tulsa Race Massacre.

Chapter Ten

An eerie panorama unfolded as we viewed the contrasting scenes of calm peacefulness in one direction and the complete devastation in another. From Cincinnati west, the beautiful morning in late spring appeared as serene and undisturbed as it could be. Not even the smoke which floated high in the air seemed to be drifting in that direction.

But looking from Detroit eastward, it was a different world. Blocks and blocks of nothing but desolate ruins. Man had wreaked in a frenzied fury to the extent of his ability. Toward the northeast, the smoke was darker, which meant that somewhere ahead of the smoke the rioters were still busy with their house burning. Down in the valley south and slightly east of Standpipe Hill, it was not possible for us to see directly north, but I was certain that the Negros homes in that direction were getting complete attention of the arson bent destroyers.

Back where the fires were first started many of them had burned out, so the smoke was white and fading away. In contrast, the high spiraling smoke was darker and darker as we again headed towards the leading edged of the hydra-headed mob. We could see clouds of dark smoke high above the north side of the hill and decided to drive far enough to the east to gain an unobstructed view in the direction. Suddenly we were aware that between us and the recently set fires to the north there was a group of maybe twenty houses that was not burning. Almost in the center of the cluster of houses was a rather large brick church and it too appeared to be undamaged.

Since smoke was spiraling into the air all around the church and group of houses, it was evident that the rioters had swerved around the undamaged buildings and continued with their burning. The situation was so unusual that we decided to drive the distance of four or five blocks and investigate the reason why the island of unburned houses and the church stood undamaged while surrounded by a sea of flames, smoke, and ashes.

We were not puzzled over the situation very long because we had not covered more than half the distance to the houses before we noticed that there were people hiding behind those nearest to us. The way they hugged the walls on the south side of the houses made it apparent that there was danger beyond. Then a number of them behind several of the houses began to wave their arms and make signals for us to stop while pointing towards the church up ahead. Our driver heeded the warning quickly.

We were just rolling into an intersection as the Indian noticed the people making the signals. He slammed on his brakes, shoved the gears in reverse, backed up about twenty feet, shifted into second gear, and tromped the gas pedal to the floor as he whipped the car around the corner and went roaring back toward Standpipe Hill. Hearing the shooting, helped him decide what to do.

Arriving at the place where the ground began to slope sharply upward toward the hill we noticed a flatbed truck blocking the street as it backed up to turn around. Forced to stop, our driver waited for the truck to finish maneuvering so we could pass.

We were impatient until the back of the truck swung around, then we noticed that on the rear of the flatbed something was mounted on a tripod and looked like a machine gun. We hesitated as we started to drive by the truck. There were three men on the truck and when one of them jerked the canvas cover from the object there was no doubt about it, a machine gun of the sort used in France in 1917-18 by the American Army was exposed. One man pulled the lid from the box and began taking belts of ammunition from it. A second man started fitting the shell belts into the grooves on the gun while a third one adjusted the sights on the gun barrel.

In seconds they were ready to fire and the man that had been adjusting the sights, turned the bill of his cap to the back, shifted into a comfortable position, aimed the machine gun toward the church, and pulled the trigger. The gun started chattering and a stream of bullets poured from the gun barrel. It soon became evident that a small amount of smoke puffed out of each shell for as hundreds of bullets flashed from the nozzle, a smokey haze surrounded the man.

The church was a little more than a quarter mile from where

the truck was located, but in a few moments, we could see chunks of mortar and bricks flying from the top part of the cupola as the bullets slammed into it. The men were firing towards the long narrow slits in the church cupola or belfry. (I never learned whether there was a bell in there or not.) But whichever it was, there were snipers up there firing through the slits and they hit some of the people as the rioters approached.

The main body of the mob had simply swung wide around the location and continued with their ransacking and burning. A rearguard formed a ring around the place by taking shelter behind the outer rim of houses and waited while a few riflemen pocked away at the snipers in the church.

I never learned how the machine gun was brought into the situation. I only know that after the snipers held off the mob for almost an hour, the machine gun came into action.

In a couple of minutes, pieces of brick started falling, then whole bricks began tumbling from around the narrow slits in the cupola. Within five or six minutes the openings were large jagged holes with so many bricks flying from that side of the cupola wall that it seemed ready to fall.

The men stopped firing the machine gun and almost immediately the houses on the outer rim of the area that had been protected by snipers, became victims of the arsonists. We watched the men take the machine gun from the tripod, wrap it in a canvas cover then lay it on the bed of the truck. They rolled up the belts with the empty shell casings, put away those that were still unused, and in what seemed less than ten minutes from the time the truck was parked at the location, drove away.

While standing on the high ground where the machine gun had been firing, we watched the activity below for a few minutes. Most of the houses were beginning to burn, and smoke ascended slowly into the air while people flitted around as busy as bees down there. From the number that ran in and out of the houses and the church, there had evidently been a couple of hundred who remained behind when the mob bypassed the area. We decided to go down and take a closer look at the damage done by the machine gun in such a short period of time.

All of the houses were burning by the time we arrived. And from the great amount of smoke pouring from the church, it was apparent that more than a fire had been started in there. Smoke was billowing out of every hole where there once had been windows. No glass remained in any of them and the bullet marks could be seen on the walls around the openings that had once been windows. Some of the spots where the bullets had splattered against the walls were two or more feet from an opening indicating that the people who did the shooting were either terrible marksmen, or they were a great distance from the church.

All the shooting around the church had stopped by the time we arrived, but after a few minutes of viewing the damaged church, which along with the houses surrounding the area was fast being consumed by fire, we became aware that shots were still being fired to the west of us. Several people were shooting into the old brick pit on the east side of Standpipe Hill. The great hole in the side of the hill was much larger than it appeared when being viewed from the top earlier in the morning,

Several years before the oil boom, the City of Tulsa had purchased the western half of the tall knoll as a location for Tulsa's water tower. The brick plant people had continued to dig the red clay from the east side of the hill to make their bricks until they reached a spot at which the city decided that any further digging would endanger the water system. When they were forced to abandon the old brick plant they moved away leaving a large deep hole with steep, craggy, crumbling red clay cliffs.

We were puzzled as to why the shots were being fired into the old pit until it was reported that several Negros were trapped in there when they were forced to retreat from the church. It was also reported that guns and ammunition had been stored in the church.

I do not know if there was a cache of guns and ammunition concealed in the church or not. Neither do I know whether the men trapped in the pit were a part of the sniper crew that had been able to escape from the church only to be trapped in the old brick plant. However, they were firing back at the members of the mob while we were watching the roof of the church collapse as the fire consumed everything flammable. It is quite possible that they were a group of Negros that fled ahead of the advancing mob and made a mistake by running into the pit.

Whatever may have happened, there were only two possibilities for them to escape from the deep hole. Either climb the eroded crumbly cliff that was probably more than two hundred feet in height or return to the opening by which they had entered and face the angry mob. Climbing the tall cliff looked impossible, yet we knew from our trip to the hilltop at dawn that a few who were unusually strong and desperate enough, had made it to the top. However, it seemed very doubtful that it could be accomplished under the conditions existing at the moment. Even if they were able to climb out of the pit, the riflemen firing at them from the eastern edge of the hole in the hillside would start trying to pick them off the wall, and at approximately three hundred yards, some of them would be able to do it. At least, anyone that tried to climb out of there was in for a heart-pounding experience.

Later we heard that about ten dead, and twenty wounded Negros were found in the pit. It was reported that there were no women or children in there with the thirty men. This might indicate that there were actually snipers from the church. If they were not snipers, why had they not been able to escape when the women and children of the neighborhood did?

A good clue as to whether they were snipers or not would have been the number of guns found in the pit with the dead and wounded Negros. If there were few guns, then it would seem improbable that the men were snipers who had just left a stockpile of weapons and ammunition at the church. Conversely, if the men were heavily armed and there being no women and children with them, one might suspect that they were actually snipers who became cut off and had to retreat into the pit.

As we stood across the street watching the church being gutted by the fire, with enough imagination, the fire that flashed out of the openings to lick along the brick walls might have been the flaming tongues of dragons.

Noticing the pock-marked wall and the distance some of the marks were from the openings, the Osage remarked, "Remember the adage about the man whose shooting was so bad that he couldn't 'hit a barn door?' Well, to judge by the distance of those bullet marks from the windows, those shooters couldn't hit the barn from inside."

Several other people were standing across the street watching as the fire roared through the church and one of them stated "I'll say one thing, the guy that was handling the machine gun certainly knew what to do with it. Look how he knocked those bricks out of that cupola!"

Another man that was standing near him added, "He not only hit the bricks with that thing, there was some dead niggers up there when he finished."

"How many bodies did you see up there?" One of the other men asked, then added "I saw four or five in other parts of the church."

From the conversation we heard, several of the group may have been the ones that set the church on fire. It also appeared that there were so many setting the fires that no one seemed certain that all of the bodies had been checked for signs of life. From what we heard it seemed reasonable to believe that there were at least seven or eight Negros bodies in the church when it was burned.

But there was so much about the affair that was indefinite, that had I not seen it burn and watched the machine gun blast the cupola, I might have thought that the entire incident was just a rumor. How many bodies were burned in that church, or how many Negros were killed or wounded in the pit, or if there were ammunition and guns stored in the church, I never learned. Nor can I say with any certainty that the Negros in the pit were a part of the church snipers who escaped from the church only to be shot later. That phase of the riot has always remained a mystery.

Chapter Eleven

I am certain that at no other time in my life have I been as hot as on the day of the riot. The warmth of a normal June day plus the heat from burning buildings caused great drops of perspiration to ooze from every pore in my body, soak my hair, and drip from the end of my nose. With eyes watering and burning from smoke and sweat, I would have gladly called my part as a spectator off and gone home, except that I hated to be called chicken by the others. And I certainly didn't relish the idea of walking through the smoking ruins, by myself, and unarmed.

Finally, the others seemed to tire of standing in the heat and smoke to watch the church burn and I gladly added my voice to the suggestion that we leave there. Driving south and back west a few blocks we passed through the section where the rioters first began their destruction. Nothing but heaps of smoldering ashes which were once buildings or houses covered the entire area. The occasional telephone or electric power pole that stood here and there with a few dangling wires, some of which were strung along the sidewalks or in the streets where they had fallen when other poles went down, seemed so out of place. Many of them were blackened and partly burned. Many of the hotlines were down and sparks flew as the wires whipped into each other earlier in the morning, but on that trip through the area, they all seemed to be dead. Evidently, the power company had cut off electricity in the Negro section.

We had decided to drive south to First Street then go east to Peoria Avenue, thereby avoiding having to pass near the burning business district from which heavy smoke erupted making visibility difficult and also because some gunshots could still be heard coming from there. We drove to the west and on south of the Negro business area for it seemed that none of us were as keenly curious about gunfire as we were a few hours earlier.

"There is a drug store a few blocks from here. Before we go back to the burning section of town and see what else the rioters have done, let's get something to drink," Harry suggested.

Everyone agreed with that idea for it had been a long hot morning. But up until then constant excitement had driven most thoughts of thirst from my mind. The suggestion of getting a drink brought the realization that I had never been so thirsty in my life.

Many times, since that day I have walked into a confectionery or drug store and the sight of a soda fountain brought memories of how relaxing and cool it was in the store by comparison with where we had been all morning. And never has anything tasted as good as the concoction of ice cream and drink mixes that I ate this morning. Feeling half-starved and overpowered by thirst, I drank and ate until reaching a state of stuffed, pleasurable misery.

A clock in the store recorded the time as 12:30 p.m. It seemed almost impossible that so much could have happened since just before dawn. The man in the drug store told us some of the things that he had heard during the morning. The city and county jails, the Convention Hall, and the baseball park were all filled with Negros that had been rounded up and herded to confinement. The National Guard Armory had been turned into a hospital and was filled to compacity with wounded Negros.

On the surface, it seemed cruel and humiliating to herd the Negros around like cattle. But under the circumstances existing at the time, I suppose it was the best thing that could be done. There were some wild-eyed killers running loose during the riot and the only reason that more Negros were not killed was that most of them fled ahead of the mob. And because those that were herded to places of safety, were gathered by persons less inclined to kill.

Driving north on Peoria Avenue, we noticed that everything to the west was totally devastated, or in the process of becoming that way quickly. There wasn't any sort of structure that was not already a heap of ashes or fast becoming one.

But to the east, smoke arose sporadically. There was much open country in that direction and the houses were most often built in clusters with open country between. We turned east off Peoria toward where some of the houses were just beginning to be set on fire. Occasionally, a single house off in the distance seemed not to be set afire. We were then beyond the city limits and also beyond any paved streets or sidewalks. In fact, the so-called streets were little more than narrow, dusty, dirt roads with weeds on either side as tall as a cow or horse, which we could barely see grazing here and there.

Noticing fresh smoke billowing up to the north, we turned in that direction on the first road that looked like it might extend that distance. The dusty road was so hemmed in with tall weeds that it was little more than a lane. Slowly, the road inclined downward from what was already low land until it reached a spot that was probably swampy in wet weather. Just ahead of us the road sloped upward slightly but since the weeds continued to close in on either side our view was restricted to a narrow slit up the dirt road.

Then we noticed that the ground began a more rapid upturn and it soon became a slight hill with a railroad crossing sign off to the side of the road. The upward slope of the ground created a knoll just high enough to make it necessary that the railroad tracks be lowered by making a cut across the top of the hill about ten feet deep to prevent an abrupt incline.

We were still about four hundred feet from the tracks when a man crouching low ran out of the weeds into the road. He glanced back over his shoulder as if expecting danger from across the tracks and stooped even lower. He made signals for us to stop but continued to glance over his shoulder making it apparent that there was danger over there.

As the roof of a building became visible a couple of hundred feet beyond the tracks the meaning of the signals the man was making became clear in a hurry. We left the car almost before it stopped rolling and ran up behind the embankment along the tracks. People were scattered out along the top peeping over to the north as others crouched in the grass and weeds fired rifles in the direction of the building.

A great many more stood at the foot of the embankment where they could stand erect without exposing themselves to the danger that threatened from across the tracks. We learned when we joined one of the groups of people standing at the bottom of the clay bank that they had been stalled for several minutes after running into the rifle fire from the building. They were waiting for riflemen because shotguns and pistols were of no use at a distance of approximately three hundred feet. A couple of times, men rolled away from the top and came down the embankment spitting dirt and wiping it from their eyes because a bullet hit the clay soil close enough to splatter them.

One of the men had been creased by a bullet just moments before we arrived. The bullet had ripped a path across his scalp just above his left ear. Blood covered his ear and trickled down the side of his face and behind the ear, soaking his shoulder and arm. He didn't seem to mind it at all for he joked and laughed with the men in his group next to us.

The stalemate at the tracks lasted for several more minutes but people continued to arrive with most of them coming up the tracks from the west. A considerable number of them had rifles and they immediately climbed up the bank on the north side of the railroad cut and began to shoot the windows on the upper floor of the building.

Suddenly a maroon-colored Marmon automobile came roaring up the dirt road from the south. Instead of stopping behind our car and the four or five that had arrived later and lined up behind it, the driver of the plush Marmon pulled out into the weeds and drove around the string of cars that had the road blocked. When it became apparent that they were not going to stop, a couple of men near the road crouched low for safety and ran out to flag down the driver of the big deluxe Marmon.

I recognized the car and the passengers. It was a group of actors from a movie studio located a couple of miles west of the Tulsa city limits. I had worked as an extra in a western picture, then had done a small bit as a Chinese laundryman only a few weeks before, so I recognized Francis Ford, the studio director, and a couple of the actors, Franklyn Farnum, and Shorty Hamilton. There was also a blond actress whose name I have forgotten, in the Marmon.

They were probably filming a picture and heard about the killing mob, so they decided to drive over and take a look at the riot. They were certainly dressed fit to kill, (no pun intended) with snow-white hats, fancy silk shirts, and loud colored bandanas around their necks, they were a sight to behold. Especially in the surrounding and under the circumstances in which they found themselves.

When they got the idea of what was going on and heard some

of the shooting, they didn't wait for further information. The driver shoved the gears in reverse, backed down the road and off down the dirt road in a cloud of dust.

Most of those who were standing near enough to realize what was happening simply broke up with laughter. One man said, "They sure didn't want to get their pretty white hats dirty did they?"

Another one laughed and added, "It didn't take them long to decide what to do after they realized that it wasn't blanks that those people were shooting."

Again, laughter greeted the remark. But remembering how quickly we had backed out of some of the situations we had stumbled into during the day, I knew just how they felt. They wanted out of there.

More and more people were coming up to join the couple of hundred that were there and quite a number of them had rifles. Waiting in safety down in the ditch which the railroad had cut through the hill, most of the new arrivals bided their time while those with rifles joined firing from the top of the bank. With the arrival of many more riflemen, the popping and cracking sounds of the different caliber rifles became continuous.

It was soon discovered that a couple hundred people had approached through the tall weeds on the north side of the tracks and were firing into the building from the west. With maybe two hundred riflemen firing from the two directions, it was only minutes before it was over. A few people went over the embankment and in seconds the stampede was on as approximately three hundred people scrambled across the tracks from the south while maybe two hundred more swarmed from the weeds to the west.

When we drove across after getting the car, smoke was already emerging from the ground floor of the building and soon it began pouring out of the openings that had once been windows on the second floor. We never heard what happened to the people that had been firing from the building, nor what sort of place or business has been above the store. It could have been living quarters, a lodge room, night club, a cheap hotel, or something else. But whatever it was, the fire put it along with the store below out of business.

There were a few houses just to the north of the store building and in moments the rioters were running in and out of them and soon they too began erupting smoke. Again, we saw no Negros around the houses. Probably everyone in the area except those who were sniping from the windows of the concrete block building had already taken flight before the rioters arrived.

While those who had appointed themselves as destroyers of the store and houses went about their business of setting them afire, the main body of the mob, continued north hunting something else to destroy. But there was little left to challenge the arsonists, and nothing to shoot.

It was perhaps half a mile from that group of burning homes to the next cluster of houses, with open country between. People were strung out the entire distance as they walked along the road. The stragglers seemed in no hurry as they plodded on toward what proved to be the end of the road and the last small group of houses. The once frenzied rioters now strolled along chatting leisurely in small groups or by twos and threes. Usually when we rolled up followed by four or five other cars, they stepped aside permitting us to pass, and many waved a friendly hand as we went by.

The leading groups of rioters were already at work on the last few houses when we arrived. Smoke was beginning to rise above them and in minutes flames broke out. And again, there were no Negros around. But off in the distance, both north and east, a considerable number of people could be seen trudging away from the city. Many seemed to have something in their hands or slung over their shoulders, but they were too far away to determine who they were, or what they were carrying. Looking off across the open country only an occasional farm home could be seen, with prairie land or small fields between them. Herds of cattle grazing on the rangeland of a few of the small ranches meant that we were quite a distance beyond the city limits.

Concentrating my attention on the people that were scattered over the countryside enabled me to conclude that those we were watching definitely were Negros who struggled to put as much distance as possible between themselves and the city. The nearest ones were at least half a mile from us while others were so far off that were merely specks bobbing up and down in the distance. I became convinced that many of those who were nearest to us were leading small children by their hands.

Those around us seemed content to stand and talk with some of them watching the refugees struggling along in the distance. Most of them had walked more than seven continuous hours as they plodded their way completely through the Negro section, burning as they went.

Starting out in the shadowy twilight just before dawn most of the mob members were filled with a feverish fanaticism and their wild, frenzied zeal, was boundless. But once having reached their goal of destroying everything that was destructible, they slowed down to a crawl. There was no place to go but back. The fire had burned out.

All over the northern and eastern part of the city and country-side there were splinter groups of what had been a giant rioting mob. As some streets ended and others zigzagged here or there, the houses were thick in some areas while sparce or clustered in others. The rioters scattered out, making every fork or turn in the streets and then into the prairies and fields hunting something to burn. Like the tentacles of an octopus, arms of the main body of the mob reached out in all directions towards the houses and buildings of every description. Even out in the edges of the city or in the country, where modern plumbing was unknown, an out-house, or privy was met and destroyed by the mob.

It was an extremely quiet ride back to the main section of the city. As we started to leave the place where the last fires were set, several people asked to ride the running boards back to town and the Indian allowed three to ride on each side of the car. We drove west on another narrow dirt road (which today is Pine Street, a wide paved avenue used by thousands of drivers going to work at the Douglas Airplane Factory, or North American Rockwell, plus heavy traffic to the Municipal Airport and many large warehous-es) to Peoria Avenue and there someone suggested that we contin-ue on west to Cincinnati then as we headed south, we could stop at Standpipe Hill and take a last look at the smoking ruins below.

The weight of eleven people put so much pressure on the springs that the body of the car was riding almost on the axles. As our driver drove along trying to avoid chug-holes in the dirt road which caused sudden jolts as the car's body banged against the axles, I looked to the north and saw more people plodding away from the city.

Some were near enough to be easily recognized as Negros carrying sacks or bundles thrown over their shoulders. Many were children who carried suitcases or bundles. But some of them so small that they had to be led by the hand while others were so tiny that they had to be carried across the fields and grassland.

Later, it was learned that more than four thousand Negros fled to the hills, creeks and the Arkansas River bottoms. Some who were fortunate enough to own an automobile or a horse drawn wagon, loaded their belongings in the vehicle and left ahead of the rioters. But those who were forced to walk, gathered what they could carry, slung the bundles across their backs and took off across country. As they fled the city, whatever they carried in those bundles had to be their entire worldly possessions.

Many who feared returning to Tulsa, made camps in the hills or along the river bottom until they could drift to other parts of the nation. A few of the camps grew into small permanent settlements. One such place is twenty-seven miles southwest of Tulsa and a couple of miles from Leonard, Okla. Leonard was one of Tulsa's satellite oil boom towns that sprang up almost overnight when the Sinclair Oil Company made a big oil strike on top of a nearby mountain in 1918.

Turning south at Cincinnati we drove as near as we could get to the top on the north side of Standpipe Hill, then walked on up to where a complete view of the Negro section was possible. When the eleven of us reached the top, we discovered that quite a number of people were already there. So many had walked around up there during the day that the tall weeds were mashed flat. There was little conversation, I guess the others were also astonished at the enormity of the devastation or couldn't think of anything to say that would fit the occasion.

I wondered about the thoughts and feelings of the six men who rode on the side of the Indian's automobile. How deeply they had been involved in the rioting, I had no way of knowing for I had never seen them before and never saw them again. But they had walked through the completely destroyed area with other thousands of people and each of the six were armed. That means that they had the equipment and opportunity, but does not mean that they committed acts of violence and since none of them offered any comment I know not what their conscience had to live with.

I have never been able to analyze my own feelings from that day very well. I believed the Sheriff when he said that there would be no charge, and that the girl admitted that she might have been mistaken, and I saw the first shot fired which touched off the riot and know that it was an accidental shot. But I also know that the couple of hundred armed men marching to the courthouse plus the other Negros speeding around town in automobiles yelling defiance, were just as wrong as could be.

But knowing most of these who had their homes and property burned or were killed, were innocent people, affected me greatly in spite of the fact that I was too young to think much about homes and families. I finally had to settle it all in my mind by being glad that we were not involved in any of the destruction, and by knowing that there was no way in which we could have prevented any of the killings or damage.

After the long period of quiet reflection, one of the nearby spectators said to no one in particular, "It is appalling. Everything has been destroyed except the earth on which the town was built. I guess that if there had been any way to set fire to the soil, it would be gone too."

Someone stated, "It is a horribly depressing sight." And I agreed, for they described the feelings that I had not been able to put into words. Maybe because I was at an age when kids are thought to be more curious than horrified at catastrophe. Whatever, I remember feeling depressed at the futility of it all.

Most of the fires in the main housing area had burned out, or nearly so, and in the business district only a few were still furnishing much fuel for the flames. More than two square miles of nothing but ashes with a wisp of smoke curling into the air here and there, except the few places in the business section where some inflammable material was buried under the debris and smoldered.

Then a lady in a nearby group noticed something that we had overlooked and said, "There is one building over there that appears to be undamaged."

She pointed toward the location. All who had heard her looked in that direction and soon agreed. There was no visible damage to a new school building.

Chapter Twelve

Strange beyond imagination, as was verified later, the almost new Booker T. Washington School was left unharmed by the destroyers. There has never been any explanation of how or why it was bypassed. Standing on the hill and surveying the devastation below it was simply unbelievable that the school had escaped damage. All other buildings, where there had once been a town of nine thousand people, were completely destroyed. Not a home, a church, a building which had housed a business, or another school had been left standing by the firebugs.

I was struck by the odd appearance of the area that had contained the better homes of the Negro section of Tulsa. The paved streets in that area looked like long strips of ribbon while those that were not paved were narrower strips or lanes with piles of grey ashes on each side. Block after block of ashes and rubbish on the streets and crisscrossing lanes created an eerie appearance.

We located the church where the shoot-out had been brought to such a quick and terrible end, by the machine gun. There was nothing left except part of a burned brick wall and some smoldering embers buried beneath piles of rubbish. Then someone in the crowd remarked, "It is amazing, but I doubt that there is one live Negro left in the entire devastated area to see what has happened to their community. What a sight will greet the survivors when they return to seek their homes. Nothing but desolation and ruins with ashes, grey and brown ashes wherever they look."

When viewing the solitary, lonely wasteland of Death Valley, with its eroded, deserted appearance of devastation, I thought back to the day I stood on the hill and viewed the desolate ruins that stood as a testimonial to man's destructive ability.

There was something majestic and awe inspiring about nature's ruins, but memory reminded me that it was the opposite when looking over the scene of man's destruction. I was much impressed by nature's work, but very much depressed by man's work of creating ruins.

Being tired to the point of exhaustion, and having a letdown feeling, I remember how glad I was when our Osage friend said, "If everyone is ready, let's be on our way."

No one objected, so we headed back to where we had left the automobile. No one felt like talking as we walked along, so we climbed in the car, and with the six men riding on the running boards, we drove toward the main part of Tulsa in silence.

As we approached First Street and Main, some National Guardsmen stopped us and told us to get off the streets because Tulsa was under martial law. The six men stepped off the running boards and went their way down the street. Our Indian friend asked if it would all right to take each of us home and the guards said, "I guess. But make it fast because everyone must be off the streets in forty-five minutes."

Guard units had arrived from all over the state, but too late to do any good. The adage about "locking the barn door after the horse was gone" seemed appropriate.

It had been more than seventeen hours since the shooting began at the courthouse and the fury of the mob was spent. Most of the rioters had either already gone home or were on their way. The schools had not opened that day, and many businesses remained closed, so it was easy to clear people from the streets. Most of them had dispersed of their own accord because the riot was over, and the weary mob had simply faded away. But for many, there was still the grieving to be done.

For seventeen hours the rioters had been neither guided, hindered, nor delayed by anything except their own moral consciousness of right or wrong, and some seemed to have little of that. Within that period of time, they had completely destroyed a city, killed between seventy and a hundred Negros, and wounded several hundred, some so critical that they never recovered.

It was fairly well established that about thirty white people were killed and near a hundred wounded. It was not possible to determine the exact number of people killed because in boomtowns the population is in a constant state of motion like the flowing and ebbing of a tide. Many come and go without being known or missed. Two things prevented an accurate count of the

Negros killed during the riot. How many were cremated in the burning buildings could not be determined, and how many of the four thousand which fled the city, never returned, was anybody's guess.

There were reports from towns and cities all over the southwest of refugees from Tulsa passing through, but the number, who knows? Also, some of those thought to have fled may have been victims of the roaring furnaces that some of the burning buildings became because of the combustible material stored in them. It must have been quite a number because some fierce fighting took place in the Negro business district. And it is very doubtful that many who stayed to fight could have escaped.

There were all sorts of rumors afloat about the amount of death and destruction that occurred in the Negro section of Tulsa. Some said that there were so many bodies not claimed or identified, and so many that were only cremated ashes, that large pits were dug, and several bodies put in each pit, creating common graves. Some of the rumors were to the effect that the city officials along with the merchants and other business leaders wanted to keep the body count as low as possible to lessen the stigma to Tulsa.

It was said that since only eleven months had elapsed between the time the hijacker was taken from the county jail and lynched by a mob, and the second mob of rioters and killers destroyed the Negro section, the big businessmen and officials were afraid that the two episodes would ruin Tulsa. Therefore, they tried to depreciate the extent of death and destruction by lowering the amount of bodies buried in the mass graves. Whether these things were all rumor and no facts, or some of both, this writer does not profess to know.

Up to this point, this has been a factual report of things seen or heard by this writer during or immediately after the riot. No research was done until now for a specific reason. I did not want my memory to be clouded by reading reports from others about incidents which I was convinced that I could report with reasonable accuracy. I must admit that in a few instances my memory may be a little hazy, but to the best of my ability, this is a true and honest report.

As odd as it may seem, there has never been a complete report written about the most destructive riot in the nation's history.[8] Several reporters for national magazines wrote an article or two, but none of them came close to writing a complete historical report of the riot. Mainly they were short garbled versions of an incident or two. It is possible that there were people who lived in Tulsa and were competent to write the history of the event, but did not desire to do so. Most everyone wanted to forget that it happened and if they witnessed any part of the riot the unpleasant memories would not induce an incentive to write about it.

Because of the poor race relations that are bringing about confrontations and building hatred and misunderstanding, I believe that it is past time for all of us to recognize how dangerous such actions are. Having once seen the terrible cost of allowing petty hatreds, rumors and confrontations to get out of hand, I realize the danger of another giant explosion happening today. The same conditions are present today which caused the riot about which this writer is narrating. Only fools think that anything is won by rioting.[9]

In continuing the recital of the known facts, the rumors that helped to bring a riot, the outcome of the grand jury investigation and the indictments issued, and the verbatim quotes of articles from six national magazines will be reported and evaluated. To the best of this writer's ability, this will be a true account of the actual happenings during the riot.

When rumors or statements in the national magazines are known to be inconsistent with the facts, the true version will be given, if known. It seemed that some of the writers for the national magazines would rather use rumors than sweat at getting the truth. Some of the articles were so asinine that they might be titled, "More Fiction Than Facts."

There were such variances in the reports about the riot by different magazines to make it seem impossible that they were writing about the same incidents. One magazine estimated the number of deaths from the riots as probably sixty-five. Another writer in an equally well-known magazine listed the number at between two hundred-fifty and three hundred dead. And yet another national publication reported that around thirty people had been killed during the rioting. (This writer saw many more thirty dead bodies.)

The amount of loss from the destruction of the Negro section, and the causes of the rioting were just as varied and distorted. This was to be expected, because the local officials and police authorities could not gather enough true evidence to put together an accurate report upon which they could agree, how would it be possible for an outside writer to come to Tulsa and gather enough facts for a correct report in a day or two?

In fact, they couldn't, and didn't. Like everyone else, they made an estimate. How accurate it was depended on how much research they did, and who they talked with about the riot. Attention will be given to those inaccurate statements when quoting the magazine items.

In researching through the files of the Tulsa newspapers, Tulsa City, County Library, Tulsa County, and Oklahoma Historical Society records, and the Hospital Medical Records Library, I found that the records concerning the riot were sparse. However, I had thirty photocopies made of items which pertained to the riot, which will be discussed in due time. By interviewing two dozen people, some of whom were contacted through advertisements in newspapers, some pertinent information was gathered.

8. A report was released in February of 2021 by the Oklahoma Commission to Study the Race Riot of 1921.

9. This manuscript was written during the 1960s and 1970s.

Chapter Thirteen

On the morning of June 2, most Tulsans awoke filled with remorse over the horrible calamity that had been inflicted on other Tulsans who were completely innocent victims of the riotous conduct of Tulsa's irresponsible element. The town has never had a reputation for doing things half-way, so when a great number of people started out to destroy the Negro section, they did so completely, and with abandon.

But as always, persons with a sense of responsibility have to repair the damage done by those who are irresponsible. And again, when Tulsa puts its shoulder to the wheel, it rolls. Thousands of people who had been involved in the rioting and destruction, still felt compassion for the victims of the riot. And realizing that most of these victims were completely innocent of any wrongdoing, they knew that there was only one way to show their concern and that was to make amends immediately.

A great effort began and a former judge, who was also a former mayor, was appointed as chairman of a large group wishing to make amends for the havoc created. They immediately started the herculean task of feeding, housing, clothing, and securing medical care for those in need. Approximately five thousand Negros were interned in the Convention Hall, city and county jails, and the baseball park. And the Nation Guard Amory was filled to capacity with wounded Negros.

An army of people, a vast amount of money and equipment was brought together and put to work attending the wounded, setting up places for the refugees to sleep and be fed. The former judge and mayor, Loyal Martin, and his reconstruction committee coordinated the efforts of all the churches, Salvation Army, Red Cross, and fraternal organizations in distributing the food, clothing, cots, tents, and other things that poured in to help the destitute Negros.

As the refugees were released from the places of internment they were temporarily housed in churches, club rooms and all sorts of buildings. And a tent city began springing up in the former Negro section. The speed with which the clearing and cleaning up of some of the ground where buildings once stood, was amazing. Of course, the help of many building contractors who volunteered their time and know-how, along with much heavy building equipment made the speed-up possible.

Along with the trucks and other building equipment came all sorts of supplies and building materials, as well as huge amounts of money. I do not know how much money was given to the individuals to help rebuild their homes and businesses, but it must have been considerable because the rebuilding went on at a fast pace.

The first consideration had to be for the health, comfort, and the convenience of the refugees who were returning by the thousands. Since the sewer and water lines were already there, it was possible to erect temporary buildings for public baths and toilet facilities in a hurry. A number of the buildings were scattered through the area for use until the land could be cleared and homes rebuilt.

With so much activity taking place in the rebuilding of the community, and with both the black and white people working so industriously side-by-side, it didn't seem possible that it had only been a few days since the place was completely destroyed because of the hatred of some members of each race for the other. It seemed impossible that martial law could have been needed only days ago.

In fact, I do not believe the martial law was needed by the time it was put into effect. If it could have been imposed eight or nine hours earlier when it was badly needed, it could have prevented many deaths and the destruction of an entire section of the city, but by the time enough force could be assembled in Tulsa to take control of the situation, the riot was over, and damage done.

When sufficient troops arrived to take charge there was nothing for them to do except prevent further trouble. It is doubtful if any more would have occurred after that because the conscience of Tulsa was busy trying to make amends for the horrible damage. Thousands of citizens of both races were engaged in reconstructing the ravaged section and a grand jury was getting ready to hold hearings to determine who was guilty of causing the damage.

During the daylight hours, the organizations that were caring for the destitute Negros worked at a furious pace and General Chas. Barrett who had put the town under martial law, did not press control so tight that it would impede the flow of assistance to the homeless Negros. But when night came, he clamped the lid tight enough to prevent any monkey business. Traffic didn't move without his permission.

Except for food and drug stores, all businesses were ordered to close at 6 p.m. and remain closed until 8 a.m. No unauthorized persons or vehicles were permitted on the streets between those hours. The only persons allowed on the streets after 6 p.m. were those engaged in activities considered to be essential to the health and welfare of the population of the city.

When Governor J.B.A. Robertson decided that the lawless period in Tulsa was definitely over, and that the responsible members of the community were in charge and rebuilding the destroyed area, he lifted martial law. But he demanded that a grand jury be called immediately to investigate the acts and conditions which caused the riot. Especially the city police department and county sheriff's office were to be checked as to their actions, or lack of action during the riot. And with the same speed that everything else was moving, the grand jury was called and went into immediate session and began issuing subpoenas and hearing witnesses.

While the jury was probing for causes and assessing responsibility for the riot, it became known that the Negro section was not the only part of Tulsa that suffered damage. When the owners of the hardware stores and pawn shops broken into by the mob had time to invoice the merchandise, they discovered that more than guns and ammunition had been taken. Heavy looting had occurred at some of them. The burglary reports listed clothing, jewelry and other things that had been stolen from the pawn shops. Some of the hardware stores had been looted of everything that could be lifted.

Many of the guns were returned after the riot was over, but some of the most expensive ones were never brought back. A number of people turned in guns at the police station reporting that they had found then in the street. In some instances, I am certain that this was true because people were afraid they would be connected to the break in and looting of the stores by possession of the guns. And in other cases, some may have felt shame and remorse over what they had done with the guns and discarded them. It is easy to support that fear and guilt complex may have caused some of them to want to get away quick, as far as possible from the guns they carried during the riot.

The fact that the grand jury was beginning to issue subpoenas for people involved in the burglaries and thefts from the stores probably helped some of the people decide in a hurry what to do with the guns. Every person that had entered one of the places broken into by the mob, even for a gun and ammunition, was guilty of a crime. No wonder that they wanted to turn loose of any evidence connecting them to the riot.

Hundreds of people were served with subpoenas, either as suspects or as witnesses to wrongful acts during the riot. Not only citizens, but policemen, sheriff's deputies, the Tulsa County sheriff, and the chief of police were called before the grand jury. Then the chief of the fire department and several of his men were served with subpoenas. It was a time of soul searching for many people.

Chapter Fourteen

Every rumor concerning the riot had to be investigated by the grand jury, and there were many. The governor assigned several state investigators to assist the jury and they were kept busy bringing in people who were connected by witnesses or rumor to some phase of the lawlessness that occurred during the rioting.

Rumors were a dime a dozen, and they were about everything imaginable. Some of them, I knew to be false the moment I heard them being spread around. One example was the different versions of what had actually touched off the shooting to the courthouse.

Rumor number one — Was a report that the shooting started when a carload of Negros rode past the courthouse and fired shots into the courthouse windows. That was as far from the truth as a rumor could get. At the time the shooting occurred there, the streets were blocked with people and it was totally impossible for an automobile to drive down either Boulder or Sixth streets.

Rumor number two — Had it reversed. It was a report that a carload of white youth drove by and fired into the courthouse. It was as preposterous as the first version and for the same reason, people in the streets. Those familiar with mob psychology will agree that rumors are the fuel that feeds the flames that causes the pot to boil over.

As stated in an earlier chapter, I was standing on the lawn at the courthouse watching and listening to the groups of approximately seventy-five, then two hundred Negros make their demand for the release of Richard Rowland and saw that first shot fired. I saw the flames shoot from the gun barrel and heard the roar as the shot was fired accidently into the air as the two men struggled for possession of the shotgun.

However, there were cars loaded with Negros circulating through the business district and driving back and forth past the police station on Second Street and waving their guns in defiance. This was one of the things brought out during the grand jury investigation. It was reported that about thirty automobiles loaded with Negros roared around town waving firearms just before the shooting started.

I am not able to attest to an exact number, but there were several cars circling in the area. And they were armed men because I saw a number of cars loaded with about all the Negros that could pile in and on them and they certainly fired pistols and shotguns at the courthouse as they sped through the streets immediately after the shooting at the courthouse began. Also, a number of windows were shot out of stores on Main Street. However, I was too busy hunting holes to crawl in to count the automobiles loaded with Negros. Also, unknown, was the number of people in those cars that were shot as they roared through town on their way back to their district.

Rumor number three — Was probably circulating in the Negro section of Tulsa some time before the day of the riot. It reported that white people wanted to scare a lot of blacks out of town because the population in that part of Tulsa was becoming so large. It was said they were taking jobs needed by the whites. Many were supposed to have been given notice to leave town by June 1. (A national magazine printed an article immediately after the riot stating the Tulsa newspapers warned the Negros to leave town)

I am certain that this was completely false. I interviewed everyone that might have any knowledge of this, and searched every record file, and could find no evidence to support this rumor. I shall quote the article from the magazine and offer more proof that it was false in due time.

Rumor number four — Was a report that a train loaded with Negros was on the way to Tulsa, from Muskogee, sixty miles to the southeast. I related this rumor earlier when reporting the walk to Midland Valley Depot, and how the mob surrounded the place to wait for the arrival of the train. Also, it was stated that the crowd hung around waiting for the train until just in time for some of them to join the large crowd waiting for daylight to start the invasion of the Negro section. But the train from Muskogee, never arrived.

The most amazing thing about this is that it was always

thought to be a rumor, but it was true. A train loaded with Negros on their way to help those in Tulsa prevent the supposed lynching of Richard Rowland, actually left Muskogee and arrived at Leonard, Okla., thirty miles from Tulsa. They were stopped there, and the train returned to Muskogee when they were told that it was too late for them to help in Tulsa because a huge white mob had already invaded the Negro section.

Only after writing more than half of this narration, did I learn that the train incident was true. I talked to several people who lived in Leonard at the time, and still do. Some of them stated that they had seen the train stopped by the passenger agent who advised the passengers on the special train to return to Muskogee because they couldn't help the Negros in Tulsa. He told them that a riot has started and thousands of white people in mobs were running the Negros out of town.

Since the train arrived in Leonard long before midnight, the full-blown riot had not started, but it is easy to understand how the confusion about conditions in Tulsa occurred. There had been shooting at the courthouse, and several Negros were killed there and in the downtown area, and they certainly were chased out of the white section of town.

The passengers on the train were lucky. If the railroad agent at Leonard had not been confused and given them the wrong information, the train would have rolled up to the depot in Tulsa to be completely surrounded by heavily armed men waiting to kill every Negro that arrived.

Rumor number five — Concerned the recruiting and agitation of the two groups of Negros which went to the courthouse to take Richard Rowland out of jail. It was reported that the editor of the Negro newspaper, the *Tulsa Star*, was deeply involved in the agitation and recruiting, and that he was sided in the troublemaking by the manager of a Negro hotel and a doctor. The rumor asserted that the three men were sending runners all over the Negro section of the city gathering guns and ammunition and taking them to the office of the *Tulsa Star* where they were distributed to those making the trip to the courthouse.

The writer does not vouch for the truth of this rumor. I do not know if the editor, doctor, or even the hotel manager had anything to do with the agitation in the Negro section. But I think it is beside the point to debate over who did the agitating and recruiting. The facts are that someone was stirring up trouble over there because all of those men didn't just happen to climb into the automobiles and go driving around in the uptown area and by the police station while waving guns in a defiant manner.

Nor did the two combined groups of approximately two hundred men, meet by accident in a sort of spur-of-the-moment, situation, and say, "Well, here we are, all meeting accidently, and all two hundred of us just happened to have our guns. Let's march to the courthouse and take Richard Rowland out of jail."

Logic tells anyone with common sense that some planned organizational effort went into getting those men, automobiles, and guns together and sending them to the white section of town to make threats. And whoever the agitators were, they did the men they recruited no favor because from having been an eyewitness, from seeing news reports, and from talking to many people who saw various parts of the action as the Negros attempted to get out of the white section after the confrontation and shoot-out at the courthouse, I can estimate that a fourth of them were either killed or wounded.

And without a doubt, that action was the number one factor in the circumstances that created the riot. And not only did the men who marched up to the courthouse pay an extremely high price for their actions, but so did thousands of innocent people in the Negro section. And if the editor, doctor or hotel manager were the agitators, they paid dearly, too because there wasn't a *Tulsa Star*, or even a building where it had been when the riot was over. Neither did the doctor have an office or a home, and where the hotel had stood, there was only ashes.

The white people didn't escape paying the Devil's toll either. Several were killed and many more wounded. Others were indicted by the grand jury and received prison sentences for their crimes after being tried in court. Conditions of anarchy does not offer a free ride for those who commit crimes.[10]

And while thousands of innocent Negros suffered along with the agitators and those who made the mistake of marching up town and threatening to burn down the courthouse if Rowland was not turned over to them, he remained safely in jail. After all of the killing and the total destruction of the district was over, Rowland was released from jail and no charges filed. Surely there is a lesson here for those who are smart enough to think.

Rumor number six — Was that in the recruiting of men to go to the courthouse and demand Rowland's release, the manager of a motion picture theater permitted the show to be stopped and speeches made to the audience about needing volunteers to go up and bring Rowland back. Also, those in the theater were supposed to have been told that who volunteered could go to the *Tulsa Star* office and guns and ammunition would be given to them.

Again, I do not know if this rumor was true or false. But as stated earlier, someone, somewhere, was doing some recruiting and agitating because the men did march to the courthouse, and they were fired up enough to take the action which ignited the fuse to the powder-keg, for I saw the explosion.

Rumor number seven — was to the effect that a doctor did not join most of his neighbors who fled ahead of the mob, but instead waited on his porch and as the vanguard of the rioters arrived, he stepped out to them and held up his arms for attention. Then as they filled the street in front of his house and his yard, he began explaining that he had done none of them any harm, and that he was a doctor, whose business was to save lives, not take them.

The second part of the rumor reported that at this point someone in the mob yelled, "What the hell are you tryin' to hand us? You are the doctor that was helpin' to agitate the whole damn mess yesterday evening. You helped gather the men that marched to the courthouse and caused all the killin'." Then he shot the doctor, the mob set fire to the house and rushed on to more burning.

There is some reference to this in the library papers, but nothing of an official nature. It was not even a newspaper or magazine article. It seemed to be merely some person quoting a rumor. Which is exactly what I am doing. I could find no information proving it was true, or a false rumor.

All rumors were checked out by the grand jury and if any proof of their veracity could be found, and a suspect, or suspects be identified, the jury issued indictments, and many were brought to justice because the investigators worked at solving whether rumors were true or false.

Many of the rumors will be noticed in the magazine articles which will be quoted in the next chapter. This writer will call attention to some them because they are so patently untrue that one wonders why they magazine reporter wasted his time with them. Of course, if they are inflammatory and helped to start the riot, then they should be reported whether true or false. The writer believes that of all the rumors floating around at the time, not more than three or four had a part in starting the riot.

10. The grand jury returned approximately 70 indictments and most of those were later dismissed. The grand jury report blamed the African Americans for inciting the riot.

Chapter Fifteen

Several national magazines rushed reporters to Tulsa to write news articles and get photographs of the destroyed area. The items in some of the magazines were so inaccurate that it was difficult not to believe that the distortions were deliberate, or that the reporters were the most inadequate that ever covered a calamitous scene. It would be easy to believe that some of the writers stayed at home and dreamed up their stories. If an article written by a reporter for one magazine is compared to one written by another for a different publication, it can be hard to believe that they were both writing about the same event.

Attention will be given to diverse statements by quoting verbatim each writer, then commenting on which one is correct if either happens to have a true report. *Scribner's Magazine* wrote about conditions existing just before, and on the evening the confrontation at the courthouse exploded into violence which began the riot:

> The negro section was rumbling with rumors at four o'clock in the afternoon. There are always agitators, and the sober, fearful members of the race have a hard time hushing them up. They tried hushing them. Grave-faced black men, ministers, church decons, real-estate owners, doctors, went to the back rooms or short-order places and pleaded with the hot-heads, 'Boys don't go over there; you'll get us burned out. You can't do any good. Don't go mixing in it. Maybe it's just talk.'

Meaning the rumors about the white people intending to lynch Richard Rowlands. And it was, with all of the talk being in the Negro section. There definitely wasn't any mob after Rowland.

Scribners' story continued with:

> 'Maybe they ain't fixing to do nothing to Jim. Don't go boys. Before God don't go over there!' But the hot-heads

were malcontents anyway. They had listened to too much imagination and too little common sense to the orators who told them that the negro was exploited and down trodden; that if he didn't assert himself, and protect his rage from the whites, what could he expect?

This writer is reasonably certain that this was fairly accurate reporting, however there was a discrepancy in Rowland's first name. How Richard became Jim is not my task to explain, I am merely quoting the magazine article which went on to say that Choc Beer may have played a part in firing up the militants. It also stated that the young men paid little attention to the pleading of the older men. Their answer was, "Let the old men mutter their hushings. They'd show the white folks that they couldn't lynch a colored boy these days. They'd show 'em. They'd see."

Scribner's ended their write-up with:

And they did see. What a truism. They saw a horrible riot with many killings, maybe relatives and friends, and their entire community destroyed.

Maybe *Scribner's* information came from interviewing some of those who tried to cool down the young hotheads, or it might have been part conjecture. Whatever the source, it was logical for I always believed that the troublemakers were few in number. But it doesn't take many to stir up a hornet's nest. Agitators always find enough followers who are dull-witted or so drunk that they don't stop and think. And those who marched to the courthouse and rode around through town brandishing their weapons and making threats, had to be unreasoning. Making demands while waving guns and threatening to burn the courthouse would be provocative in any city. In Tulsa, it was like playing with matches in a powder house.

Survey Magazine, published in New York City, only ten days after the riot, came out with an article entitled, "Blood and Oil." This story contained more misinformation than facts. It reported that large groups of Negros had fled Tulsa three weeks before the riot because the Tulsa newspapers on three successive days had printed warnings for them to get out of town. It stated that the newspaper warned the Negros that their population would be thinned down by June.

I do not claim that the reporter who wrote this garbage misused his expense money intended for his transportation and expenses while gathering information about the riot in Tulsa, but had I been the publisher of that magazine, I would have checked all of the opium-dens near New York City to see which pipe that dream came from.

That statement was simply not true. I was certain of this before doing any checking for facts, and after much research through the history of Tulsa, microfilmed files in the newspaper offices, Tulsa City, County Library, and talking to retired police officers, firemen and newspaper people, I can state that beyond the shadow of a doubt that the story was false.

If such warnings for the Negros to get out of town had been printed, it would have been clear evidence of inciting a riot and the grand jury would have issued an indictment. Also, the Negro property owners could have owned the newspapers by filing damage suits for the destruction of their property. The "leave town notices" part of the story was a pipe dream.

The *Survey Magazine* story was filled with false information:

> No explanation was given for the warning, which was repeated on unsigned cards pasted on the doors of Negro homes. But nine were needed, since the attitude of certain whites (*sic*) and the reason for the warning were well known.

The magazine offered the reason for the warnings as the well-known jealousy by the whites over the jobs being taken by the Negros which the whites wanted. The entire idea of jealousy over jobs will be refuted by quoting from another magazine, but first the warning story needs to be explained, and I believe that I may have been given the answer by a stranger.

After writing everything I could remember as having seen or heard during the riot, research was started. Every known source was checked for any possible piece of information that might add truth and understanding to this report of the riot. Then after checking libraries, newspapers files, and historical society records, and interviewing every person I know that might remember any incident, I decided on one more attempt at getting other information.

I ran advertisements in the newspapers asking that any person having any information about the Tulsa riot, contact me. Several people did, and I gained some knowledge in this manner, also about a dozen photographs of the various phases of the riot were loaned for me to have copies made.

During a couple of long talks, one man offered a very plausible explanation for the garbled warning story. He said, "You know, I might just know where the magazine got that story. Several months before the riot, it might have been as much as a year before, there were some pretty bad "niggers" over there. Maybe not many, but there were some bad ones there. Crooked gamblers, pimps, bootleggers, hijackers, and burglars hid out over there and worked over that part of town as well as the white section.

The bootleggers weren't above selling water in a bottle to some of the boys who came in from the drilling rigs. And the nigger pimps had their whores hustling at night over across the tracks. They walked along Archer, Boston, and Cincinnati and all the places where the edges of the white and black sections of town joined. That part of town was quite dark at night and not the safest place to be after dusk."

I remembered that the "red-light" district of Tulsa was in that area during the early boom days. I had heard that it was a real tough neighborhood at that time. Only fourteen or fifteen when my family moved to Tulsa, I was a little young to be interested in the business conducted in the area during that period. But I was aware that even though there was no longer a "red-light" district, as such, at the time of which the man was speaking, it was still a dangerous place.

The man who had answered my advertisement continued, "If a person was drunk, or foolish enough to stop and talk with the hustling gals in the shadowy, dimly lighted area, he soon found himself being worked over real good. The gal would be all over him in a minute with her body pressed tight against his as she squirmed and felt around on him until she had him excited. If he was foolish enough to be coaxed into a dark alley, or into the shadows of a billboard, what he most often got, was not what he expected."

Listening with much interest, I thought the man spoke as if relating some personal experiences, but he didn't say how he gained the knowledge of conditions he described:

Usually, the hustlers tried to find out if a man had more money than they could get in the classical manner. If not, they sold him a few minutes of their time, collected their money, and let him go on his way. But, if a gal thought her victim had more money, she worked on him until she knew that he was steamed up like a locomotive, then suggested, 'Honey, I need a drink. I can get some real cheap next door. I'll go get it and you can give me a few dollars when I return. If you will do it, then I'll take you back here in the dark and show you the best time you ever had.'

If he went for her deal, she then told him that she wanted to be sure that he had enough to pay for her time and the drink. If he was stupid enough to flash a fair sum of money, she went to get the whiskey. She returned to inform him that she had it and coaxed him back in the darkness by saying they couldn't have a good time where it was light enough for people to see them.

When he walked back into the shadows with her, most often it was to be banged on the head with a brick in the hands of her pimp. Then he revived to find that the nigger hustling gal, her pimp and his money were gone.

I didn't see any connection between the story the man was telling and the warning in the newspapers for the Negros to leave town but decided that he was trying to lay the background for his theory and I didn't interrupt.

He added:

Several men were hurt by black hijackers too. Stepping out the shadows in the white section, they used a gun, or knocked someone in the head to rob him. And the nigger burglars pulled jobs up town too.

The Ku Klux Klan had been putting the cure to several white criminals, so they started whipping a few blacks too. Then one night, they posted notices on the doors of several undesirable people, both white and black, telling them to leave town, or have their hide torn off and replaced with tar and feathers. I seem to remember that the newspapers printed the story about the Klan posting the notices for those people to leave town.

It sounded like the man knew what he was talking about, but again, I didn't ask if the information was straight from the horse's mouth, for he refused to allow me to identify and use his name as my informant. However, what he narrated was so logical that I believe it to be the answer to the warnings in the newspapers story.

If this was true, *Survey Magazine* missed the target by miles. What the newspapers had printed was that notices had been posted warning the Negro criminals to leave town and the same warnings had been issued to those in the white section. The notices by the Ku Klux Klan had nothing to do with there being jealousy over jobs, nor about the Negro population becoming so large that some of them had to be scared out of town. That *Survey* story was a garbled version of poor reporting.

My informant related another incident that probably caused some of the resentment which made it easier for the agitators to fire up the Negros and make some of them easy victims for the orators to manipulate into making the trip to the courthouse which touched off the riot:

> Not long before the Klan sort of gave-up-the-ghost and began to fade away, they cut a nigger's ear off. I don't remember why, but they sure did cut it off. I don't remember if they were supposed to have ordered him to leave town either. If they did, they may have forgotten about it because the Klan was having problems of their own along about that time. I believe that it happened just a year or two before the riot.

That was the end of the narrator's description of conditions and incidents around the time that the riot occurred.

But as he related the incident about the Negro man's ear, my memory began to recall a rumor in connection with a Negro that I became acquainted with twenty years after the riot. He was a police officer and had been on the force around fifteen years when we met. He was minus one ear, and another officer informed me that it had been cut off during Tulsa's early days by the Ku Klux Klan.

Even after knowing the Negro officer rather well for a number of years, I still never learned the details regarding the loss of his ear. He never mentioned it, and people respected his desire not to discuss it. But I heard several times that it was done by the Klan.

He remained a respected member of the Tulsa Police Department for more than twenty years, then retired.

Never having heard of any reason for the ear incident, I will make no conjecture about it, except to say, there may not have been a reason. From all I ever heard about the Klan, there were some real haters in that thing, and some didn't care if they could find a reason or not to vent their anger upon those they considered undesirable, especially Negros and Jews.

I explained when relating the tar and feather incident, that the Klan began to disperse at about the same time as mentioned by the narrator of the ear incident. But fear and resentment were already rampant in the Negro section.

Chapter Sixteen

Approximately five hundred Negros owned land in the state of Oklahoma and oil was discovered on several of the farms and ranches. *Survey Magazine* made another error in asserting that jealousy over the few Negros owning oil wells was a large contribution to the riot.

This I do not believe for two reasons; first, because I can't recall ever hearing one person mentioning anything that indicated jealousy over the Negro ownership of oil wells. Second, not one oil storage tank, or oil well was destroyed by the rioters. And although most of them were a few miles from town, a couple of automobiles loaded with rioters could have driven there, destroyed the wells and been back to town in a couple of hours.

Quoting more of the inaccurate reporting by *Survey Magazine:*

> Every increase in the price of oil made the strife more bitter. With the depression of the labor market, white employers of labor at last thought they had the whip hand and ordered the negro employees to sell out or quit. Even housewives refused to continue colored women in their employ. Petty persecutions, the refugees say, were common, though there had been no physical violence for years. Then came the alleged attempt of a negro mob to prevent the lynching of a colored man who was held in jail on charge of assault on a white women, white men and boys from every part of the city on June 1 armed themselves, raided sports goods and hardware stores for more arms and ammunition and staged a riot in which thirty persons, majority colored were killed.

There was far more misinformation in the *Survey Magazine* write-up, which is quoted verbatim, then there was accurate information. Having followed the first group of marching Negros to the courthouse and being there on the lawn when the second group arrived and threatened to burn the courthouse if Rowland was not released, I can state it was not an "ALLEGED" group of Negros which came there. Although the Negros probably thought they were there preventing a lynching, there wasn't one planned. There wasn't a white mob there, in fact not more than thirty of us who followed the Negros out of curiosity were on the lawn during the first ten or fifteen minutes.

It was at least three hours after the shooting at the courthouse before the hardware stores and pawn shops were broken into and the crowd became an armed white mob. And as for the thirty people being killed, that figure was so unreal, that it was ridiculous. Including those killed in the courthouse area and in the streets of the business district as the negros fought their way towards their part of town, the young man at the freight depot, and the five men in the Franklin automobile, I saw at least that many bodies. And others were seen throughout the Negro section. There were dozens of others unseen that were burned in the church and business buildings. Besides, our spectating could have covered only a small part of the total riot. I will quote from other national magazines which list the number of deaths as several times that stated in *Survey*, but first a telegram from a Tulsa editor.

Richard Lloyd Jones, editor of the *Tribune* (If I remember correctly, it was then called the *Tulsa Democrat*) sent a telegram to the *New York World* which published the news of the Tulsa riot and quoted a part of the wire from the Tulsa editor as its source. I quote the *New York World*:

> As is too often the case in just such situations, the police are derelict of duty at the psychological moment when they have the power to prevent. As soon as this small band of armed black men came upon the scene, the Tulsa Police, with or without the aid of county officals, should at once thrown a line around them and marched them off to jail. (the first seventy-five Negros that we followed to the courthouse) But they stupidly let the psychological moment pass. Then a white man struck a match to the incendiary mob-power by trying to take a gun away from a negro.

This is verification of my statement as an eyewitness to the accidental shot being fired as the two men struggled over the shotgun.

On June 15, fifteen days after the riot, *Outlook Magazine* printed a story about the riot entitled "The Lesson of Tulsa." It began by printing a newspaper dispatch from Tulsa:

> On the night of June 1, a newspaper dispatch from Tulsa, Oklahoma, said, The hospitals of Tulsa are filled with wounded and dying men tonight and the morgues are crowded with the dead after twenty-four hours of rioting between white men and negros.

This sounds like more than thirty total deaths. *Outlook Magazine* stated that it had telegraphed a "Well-informed Western Correspondent," to proceed to Tulsa to get the full story of the Tulsa riot. But to continue with *Outlook's* first article and its attempt to identify the causes of the riot. The magazine quoted a statement made by General Barrett to the Tulsa newspapers while the town was under martial law.

When asked his opinion as to the cause of the riot, he stated that it was caused, quote, "by an impudent negro, a hysterical girl and a yellow journal reporter."

The magazine editorialized:

> It may be said that this horror was caused by the misuse of a word; it was reported that a white girl had been 'assaulted' by a colored man; the fact was, it now appears, that a bootblack stepped on an elevator girl's foot, that she slapped him, and he grasped her by the throat.

Because of the great length of the article sent in by the western correspondent which *Outlook Magazine* printed, I will not quote all of it. Besides, seventy-five percent of it dealt with rumors and incidents which have been discussed from every angle already. The opening paragraph was certainly relevant:

> Tulsa, the scene of the recent rioting, is an Oklahoma oil city of mushroom growth. It has a population of seventy-three thousand, of whom perhaps eight thousand are Negros. The Negros are employed chiefly in forms of service not sought by whites. Day laborers; the women cooks, charwomen, laundresses. There has been no industrial race friction.

How does that match the statement in *Survey Magazine*, that jealousy over jobs was a factor in causing the riot? The writer in *Outlook Magazine* made much sense in the next paragraph too:

> What is the significance of the tragedy for the rest of the nation? Tulsa is not essentially different from any American city in which there is a considerable Negro element. Contemplating the dark episode, almost any other city might echo the humble thanksgiving, 'But for the grace of God there goes John Bunyan.' So long as race feelings exist there is danger of such outbreaks. Depreciate it all we please, the foundations of order are secured theough effective police enforcement backed by a firm demand for law and order by all decent citizens and helped by the earnest desire of white and colored people ro draw togather in just and friendly relations.

The person who wrote the above for *Outlook Magazine,* said a big mouthful. His closing paragraph was also pertinent:

> In the long run, civilization must depend on the education, tolerance, and intelligence of the mass of the people. But, as the experience of Tulsa and so many other cities shows, police forces cannot be demoralized by politics or by neglect exceot at the risk of disaster.

One June 18, eighteen days after the riot, *Independent Magazine* published an article with some flaws. However, the writer did a rather good job because most of it was factual. It too, refutes the statement by *Survey,* that jealousy over jobs was a factor in the conflict:

> No riot ever struck a city with less warning or found local authorities less ready to cope with it. It was a spontaneous flare-up based on old prejudices, new suspicions, and wild rumors. A Negro was arrested on the charge of attacking a white elevator girl in an office building. Although he was held safely in prison awaiting trial, the rumor spread that there would be a lynching. The Negros thought the report probable enough, and, without waiting to investigate the truth, they assembled an armed band of serveral hundred men around the courthouse to protect the prisoner. The police attempted in vain to disperse the mob of blacks, a number if shots were fired.

The preceding paragraph was factual until near the end, then it bogged down with guesses instead of researched truths. It was the sheriff and a Negro deputy that tried to get the Negros to disperse and return home, not the police. I will stand by my estimate of two hundred, instead of the reported several hundred Negros in the courthouse crowd. And the effort to disarm the Negro was by one man.

The following paragraph puts the assembling of two mobs in their proper sequence and verifies my statement that the white mob began forming after, and as a result of the Negros marching to the courthouse:

> Then another mob assembled, a white mob. Whether it had originally planned a lynching or not, it was now bent on mischief. The whites were inadequately armed, so they broke into hardware and sporting goods stores and took what rifles, shotguns, revolvers, and ammunition they could lay hands on. Many of them rode unchallenged thru the streets with arms in hand.

> After a consderable amount of sniping, the negros around the courthouse were beaten back. By dawn on June 1, the whites were in command of the situation. Neither the police department nor the sheriff took any effective steps to stop the activities of the two rival mobs. At daybreak the troubles took on a new and more sinister phase. No longer content with the negative victory of having driven the blacks into the negro quarters, the white rioters decided to carry the war, into enemy country.

The long item continued with a description of the invasion and destruction, but that has been described before, besides, the two proceeding paragraphs are the message bearers, they teach the real lesson to those who will read and think. What happens when law and order break down was vividly shown during the Tulsa riot. Yet, today, we hear foolish young militants of all races preaching anarchy as if it was a desirable condition.

Another national magazine reached the news-stands and bookstores on June 18. *Nation Magazine* printed a long recital about the riot by Walter F. White, entitled, "The Eruption of Tulsa." Mr. White repeated all of the dozen or more rumors as causes of the rioting. To list all of them would take several pages and be repetitious, but Mr. White did offer one situation as contributing to the riotous conditions that the other writers didn't mention:

> A vice ring was in control of the city allowing control of houses of ill fame, of gambling joints, illegal sale of whiskey, the robbing of banks and stores, with hardly a possibility of the arrest of the criminals. And even less of their conviction.

I will not debate over Walter White's allegations. There is always the possibility that his assertions were true. But some doubts are raised by the fact the in no other place did I hear of such conditions during my research and interviews. Besides, I can't understand how such a condition would have contributed to creating the riot. I believe that the writer was floundering on uncertain ground in part of the following narration also:

> A hysterical white girl related that a nineteen-year-old colored boy attempted to assault her in a public elevator in a public building of a thriving town of 100,000. Without pausing to find out whether or not the story was true, without bothering with the slight detail of investigating the character of the woman who made the outcry, a mob of 100-per-cent Americans set forth on a wild rampage that cost the lives of fifty white men; between 150 and 200 colored men, women and children; the looting of many homes; the destruction of $1,500,000 worth of property; and the everlasting damage to the reputation of Tulsa and the state of Oklahoma.

Mr. White was a bit high on his estimation of fifty white men and a hundred and fifty or two hundred Negros being killed in the riot. About twenty-five or thirty whites and seventy Negros would have been more realistic. Those who were best informed agree that the damage was around $2,000,000, a huge amount at the time,

But reporter White really stepped into the quicksand when he criticized the police for the arrest of Rowland. Without bothering with the slight detail of investigating the character of the woman who made the outcry. It is apparent that Walter White did not understand the laws of arrest. The police have no authority to investigate any person until either a warrant for the arrest has been issued, or there is sufficient evidence indicating that it is reasonable to believe that the person has committed a felony. Besides, if the police took the time to investigate the character of every person who issued a complaint before seeking the suspected felon, half of the murderers would be in South America when the search for them began. Also, under law, every person, whether they are black, white, Democrat, Republican, Baptist, Methodist, Catholic, banker, doctor, or just a skid-row bum, has a right to file a complaint and seek justice if a crime against them has been committed. Even a streetwalking prostitute has a right to file a complaint if she has been beat up, robbed, or any other type crime has been committed against her.

There is nothing under the law that says that because she is a prostitute, she may be mistreated with impunity. Only the courts can decide after a hearing, if the complainant's reputation or character has any bearing on the case. Criticizing something of which we have no knowledge, is typical.

In his story for *Nation Magazine* on June 29, almost a month after the riot, Walter White closed with a paragraph which also refuted the theory about the riot being planned in advance:

> This in brief, is the story of the eruption of Tulsa on the night of May 31, and June 1. One could travel far and find few cities where the likeihood of trouble between the races was as little thought of as in Tulsa. Her reign of terror stands as a grim reminder of the grip mob violence has on the throat of America, and the ever-present possibility of devasating race conflicts where least expected.

The relevancy of the above to conditions today, is startling. Agitators, and hate-mongers, are preaching violence and destruction to the extent of complete anarchy. By alerting people to the horrors committed under conditions of lawlessness, it is hoped that they will refuse to follow the preachers of anarchy and violence. Without followers to do their dirty work, agitators would be like a cannon without ammunition, a big mouth, but no damage. This is the real motive for writing this narrative of the Tulsa riot. By "telling it like it is," maybe some will understand and avoid becoming victims of the peddlers of death and destruction.

Students from the universities of Tulsa, and Oklahoma, while working on degrees, have done considerable writing and research about the Tulsa riot. I came across several while seeking information for this recital. One thesis written by a student who was a candidate for a master's degree, wrote:

> At 8:30 a.m. the advancing cordon came upon a group of Negros in a church and a group of residences in a small valley at the foot of a hill. The whites were met with heavy fire, killing one white and wounding several others. Reinforced by a machine gun they again advanced. The negros held out until the machine gun riddled the chruch and set it afire. The negros retreated leaving fifty dead or wounded lying in the valley.

Obviously, this concerned the machine gun incident which we discovered when the truck blocked the street as it was turning around to aim the gun at the church. Comments are unnecessary except to say that I believe that the time was a little later, maybe nearer 9:30 a.m. And I can only repeat the rumor we heard about the number of dead and wounded Negros in the brick-pit. There were forty or more people standing around watching the church burn, and some of them said that about thirty snipers from the church were trapped in the pit.

One University of Tulsa student who was doing research for a paper while working on his master's degree, ended his thesis with the statement:

> Perhaps the memory of the black day should be left alone, but its lesson should not be forgotten.

Until recently it had also been the belief of the writer that this ugly chapter in Tulsa's history should remain closed. This is no longer true because every day the news media is filled with reports of racial frictions, and about acts of violence, and anarchy. City after city reports such things as 400 rock-and-bottle throwing youths had to be dispersed by the police after a second night of violence in Jacksonville, Fla. Or about the arson and sniper fire that occurred in Chattanooga, Tenn. Or, from New York City one reads, quote, "The ambush shooting of two police officers in New York City holds the potential trouble that could turn into a horrible tragedy." The news item states that for three days police officers were assailed.

A clincher on how serious the agitation for trouble has become, is that it is happening in Chicago, New York City, Washington D.C., Miami, Cleveland, Detroit, Newark, Los Angeles, and dozens of other cities. In fact, a real "Donnybrook" took place in New Orleans. All of the details are not yet known, but a sniper, or snipers, shot about a dozen people, killing several including a high-ranking police official and other police officers. Even firemen were shot while trying to extinguish a fire in the eighteen-story building. One was picked off while climbing a ladder.

I am guessing 95% of those incidents of death and destruction have one thing in common, agitators are exploiting the youth and inexperience of their followers. About 2% of the nation's young people are committed to the destruction of constituted authority and creating anarchy. Approximately 3% of the young people follow the agitating troublemakers because they believe it is the, "in-thing," to do. Totally unaware that they are used as dupes and stooges.

It is not just the SDS, Dubois Society, Panthers, and Weathermen[11] groups that are appealing to the young to follow. Freelance anarchists are hunting puppets who will dance when their strings are pulled. And not all of the hate-mongers are young militants. The Ku Klux Klan is trying very hard to raise its ugly head again.

Only fools believe that conditions of anarchy are desirable. It means a breaking down of all rules of government, a totally lawless condition in which nothing is forbidden. There is nothing to stop, delay, or even hinder the most cold-blooded acts of murder, robbery, arson, or rape. If anarchy lasts long enough, every person becomes its victim. There is nothing except the conscience of each person to stop the murderous action, and a criminal has no conscience, and neither does a mob.

11. The author is referring to some groups of the era that were at times considered radical. Here he mentions Students for a Dempcratic Society (SDS), W.E.B. Dubois Society, Black Panthers, and Weathermen.

Chapter Seventeen

The order by governor J.B.A. Robertson declaring martial law in Tulsa County was received by Adjutant General Chas. Barrett at the National Guard Armory on June 1, at 11:29 a.m. By the time enough guardsmen could be called to duty from all over the state, transported to Tulsa and then deployed, it was about 2 p.m. Finally, the barn door was closed, but the horse was gone.

In the late afternoon people began calling the Tulsa Police Department, or the Tulsa County Sheriff's office trying to locate, or learn the fate of their employees that had not been heard from since the day before. Finally, a listing of those who were interned in the jails, the Convention Hall, and in the baseball park, was compiled and when someone called about a missing chauffeur, maid, cook, or gardener the list was checked, and the caller was advised where to go to secure the release of their employee. Many called in vain, because the employee was among those who fled Tulsa or had been killed.

Someone decided that as the Negros were released from interment, a yellow band should be tied around their arms to indicate that he or she, had been properly released. Some of the released employees were back at work chauffeuring or gardening with yellow bands on their arms. Which seemed rather silly since the internment had been only for their own protection and once released that should have ended it. There had not been any criminal charges filed as yet against anyone. Some may have been filed later when the grand jury finished their investigation and issued indictment. At the time of internment no charges had been filed against any person and it was not yet known who had committed crimes, either black or white.

When a doctor called regarding his chauffeur, he was advised to go to the baseball park because his employee's names appeared on a list of the twenty-five hundred Negros entered there. When the doctor arrived there seeking the release of his chauffeur, he discovered a couple of dozen white men were acting as guards, check-off men, or those who went inside the ballpark to bring out those to be released. The men seemed to be volunteer workers, so it was quite possible that they had appointed themselves to those capacities.

The person who related the incident to me, said:

> The chauffeur was about forty years of age and he was released to the doctor, it was apparent that they were on friendly terms. The moment the Negro walked through the gate and saw the doctor, he grinned happily. The doctor smiled as he walked over and offered his hand, which the Negro took in a firm grasp. After shaking hands, the doctor asked, 'Are you alright George?' They turned to leave, and the doctor put his arm around the Negro's shoulders and inquired, 'They didn't hurt you, did they George?'
>
> Then a large bull-necked man who badly needed a shave stepped from the crowd of several men standing near the gate, grabbed the doctor's arm, spun him around and hit him in the face with a huge fist that covered chin, mouth, and nose. The doctor went sprawling and was bleeding heavily as he staggered to his feet and took a handkerchief from his pocket to cover his bleeding face. The big man with the appearance of an oilfield roust-a-bout, said, 'You damn nigger lover!'
>
> Then something happened that seemed so ludicrous, considering all of the happenings of the last 24 hours. Two police officers drove up in time to see the doctor getting up with blood flowing from his nose and mouth. They walked over and asked what had happened and when informed about the large man had struck the doctor, they asked, 'Sir, do you wish to file charges against the man that hit you? If you do, we will take him to the station.' The doctor shook his head no and walked away.

The person relating the incident said that it seemed so odd that after all the killing and burning the police offered to arrest the man for striking someone with his fists. But this simply proved that everything was back to normal, and law and order had returned.

The incident pointed out another thing that had caused the wild, excessive violence that occurred during the riot. Blind prejudices and hate had been the impelling forces that created the riot, and still lingered in such people as the man who struck the doctor. Race hatred seems to be just beneath the surface in quite a number of people, both black and white. Those who are the lowest in academic achievement, and nearest the bottom of the economic scale, are the greatest haters.

The same informant related another incident that had a bearing on the creation of the riot. I had always thought that the five of us who were singing on the school grounds had seen and followed the first group of Negros that came up town to protect Rowland from what they believe to be a hanging. But the second person to answer my newspaper advertisement for information about the riot, convinced me that I was mistaken. And is further proof that the agitation was hot and heavy in the Negro section long before dark. He stated:

> I was standing on Main Street in the afternoon of May 31, when a group of approximately forty negros carrying weapons approached from the north. They were marching right down the center of the street and had almost reached Third Avenue when a white man stepped off the curb and walked beside the large negro while conversing with him for a moment.
>
> Suddenly the white man pulled a revolver from a holster on his hip and pointed it in the center of the large negro's stomach. They had arrived at a position directly in front of me, so I heard the man very clearly as he took a badge from his pocket, showed it to the negro man and said, 'I am a deputy sheriff. Stop these men right now.' The big man turned and held up his hand and they all stopped. Then the deputy said to them, 'I am sworn to enforce the law and you are violating it by coming up here with those guns. Either you turn around and head back or I am going to empty this revolver, two shots in your belly and the rest in the men nearest to me. Some of you may shoot me, but if you do, you will all hang. Go back where you came from or a

lot of us will die right here.' He looked small standing beside the negro leader, but I have never seen a man with so much guts.

When I mentioned having been told of this by one of my brothers, he said:

I remember that. It was so long ago that I had forgotten it. I didn't see it all, but (he mentioned the names of two boys of his age who were neighbors at the time) were with me and when we started to cross Main Street, we noticed a crowd standing along the curb watching a group of negros with guns.

"Then we saw a white man standing with his gun pointed at the stomach of a negro man. The other negros with guns in their hands stood there watching as if waiting to be told what to do. The thing I remember the clearest about the incident was how odd it seemed that the negros all turned around and headed back north, while the white man stood in the street and watched for a moment, then put his pistol back in its holster and stepped to the curb to join the crowd that lined the street watching as the negros marched back home. None of the negros even turned to glance back.

My brother remembered that the time was somewhere near 5 p.m. when the Negros marched back to their section of town. This was around two and half, maybe three hours, before the armed group went marching past the high school where we sat singing harmony.

It is positive proof that someone was doing some long and determined agitating over in the Negro area. The recruiting had to continue for hours because the armed groups continued to appear in ever increasing numbers for some time. At least up until the second time the group arrived at the courthouse, which was at approximately 8:30 p.m. This became an established fact because each time an assembly of Negros appeared up town, it was a much larger group than the one before.

In spite of the danger involved, some person or persons continued to heat-up conditions by sending groups of armed negros for confrontations. With each arrival making the situation a little more tense, an explosion was bound to occur. When the forces of law and order did not move immediately to deter these violations, others were almost certain to follow. When the other side countered with violations, a sort of "tit-for-tat" situation developed.

Inevitably the question arises as to the part rumors played in creating riotous conditions. They must have been the fuel with which the agitators stoked the flames. Because whether a cause is good or bad, right or wrong, there is never a shortage of agitators or fuel to feed the furnaces of race hatred.

The rumor that Rowland was going to be lynched by a white mob was the number one cause of the riot because the agitators in the negro section used it to arouse their followers. They probably accepted it as a fact, although it definitely was not true. The extent of the agitation was not lessened by the fact that the entire affair was mixed up or garbled as to what had actually happened between Rowland and the girl operating the elevator.

The first knowledge the white part of town had of the mixed-up story about Richard Rowland trying to assault a white girl in an elevator, came when the midday newspaper printed the story on May 31, and called it an attempted rape. It stated that the attempt had occurred the previous afternoon and that the police had arrested Rowland who was now being held in jail.

The fact that the news report stated that it was only an attempted rape and that Rowland had already been arrested, prevented any real excitement in the white section of town. But because the police were seeking him in the negro district since the night before, plenty of time was allowed for rumors to build.

Although the shooting at the courthouse which triggered the riot was accidental, the actual violence which erupted there must be charged to the two hundred armed negros who believed the rumor enough to assemble in lawless defiance and created conditions for the riot. It made no difference that they were gathered there because of agitation over a false rumor, when they met there and threatened to burn the courthouse, no other excuse was needed for the white agitators to shift into high gear.

Chapter Eighteen

The grand jury was called and began its hearing on June 17, 1921, just seventeen days after the riot. It issued subpoenas, began hearing witnesses and investigating rumors immediately. Several hundred people were called to appear before the jury, both black and white.

It must have been about the busiest grand jury in history. Seven days after it started issuing subpoenas and hearing witnesses, indictments for the arrest of persons charged with crimes were returned. Thirty white men were arrested on indictment, charging rioting and vandalism. Many others were charged with looting or grand larceny during the riot.

Sixty-four negros were indicted at the same time for rioting. One white man and one negro were charged with inciting a riot. All of this occurred on the seventh day after the grand jury went into session. This was not the end of the indictments. They continued until the jury issued its final report.

This was a period of real excitement for most Tulsans. For many others, it was a time of fear because the truth about how the riot created, and who started it, was now being revealed by the indictments. It was a time of soul searching for many people. As new subpoenas called more people before the jury, those who were guilty of crimes must have had some anxious moments. Would the axe still fall? Would their names come up during the investigation?

Another person indicted by the grand jury was Chief of Police Gustafsen. He was charged with neglect of duty. With failing to take positive action to prevent the riot. The jury's report said that he should have used the entire police force if necessary to corral the first group of negros that came marching down the street brandishing weapons illegally. And that the negro occupants of the automobiles that were speeding up and down the streets in defiance of the law, should have been arrested the moment they appeared. The report stated that no such orders were ever issued to the police. The report concluded by charging Chief Gustafsen with being too permissive on gambling and prostitution.

As a result of the grand jury investigation and indictments, fifty-six Negro plaintiffs who had lost property because of the riot, filed damage suits against the Tulsa city officials. They charged the city officials with having entered into a conspiracy with numerous unidentified persons to deprive the Negros of life, liberty, and their property.

Only one of the suits was ever tried. It was dismissed for lack of evidence. The Negro could offer no evidence of a conspiracy. His attorney admitted that they had no witnesses to prove that the officials were in any way connected with the riot. Nor did they have the name of any person who conspired with the city officials. The court ruled that no conspiracy existed and dismissed the case. Attorneys for the other fifty-five plaintiffs also dismissed the charges because they could find no evidence to support their charges.

Even though many indictments were issued, it is quite possible that there were far more persons guilty of crimes than were ever indicted. But the jury could only use such information as was presented to it. When testimony during their investigation implicated some person, a subpoena was issued and if there was evidence to support a charge, an indictment was issued. Considering the great amount of people involved, and the reluctance of most people both white and black to admit knowing anything about the riot, the jury did a remarkable job.

It is not the purpose of the writer to assess responsibility for the riot. There was great wrong done on both sides. The negro agitators were probably guilty of instigating the incidents that started things moving when they recruited the armed men. Their agitation excited the men enough to go to the courthouse and take the action that lit the fuse which brought about the explosion.

But there was agitation on the other side too. Retaliation became the theme, and once it was started, the excesses were not only unreasonable, but unbelievable. There were many who seemed to feel that only total extermination and destruction of the section would be satisfactory. Only the fact that most of the Negros had fled ahead of the mob, and that the self-appointed exterminators were hampered in their efforts by the more reasonable majority, prevented a lot more killing. Most of the people seemed to feel that only those who shot at the white people should be killed.

I do not claim that my interpretation of what I believe were the feelings of the rioters are facts. It was simply my impression that a majority of the people involved in the riot were less inclined to extreme violence than some of the others. I also believe that at least twenty percent of the crowd were spectators only. Not actually involved in the riot but did the same as the five of us who followed the rioters through the approximately six-hour period that the invasion of the Negro section lasted yet remained strictly sideline spectators to the end. Our only participation was in three instances. Twice when we were talked into taking the groups of Negros to the station for their own protection. And when we took the two wounded Negros to the hospital.

I stated that I believed that the grand jury did an excellent job under the circumstances which existed at the time. When the jury's final report was released, it showed what an exceptionally good public service it had performed. In addition to the rumors that were listed earlier as having played a part in creating the riot, there were a dozen others floating around. The jury had to investigate each of them to determine whether they were true or false before indictments could be issued.

Some of the most damaging and trouble causing incidents were completely false. The one that really blew-the-lid-off, was false; that a white mob was waiting to lynch Rowland. In fact, under conditions of great stress, false rumors may be the most dangerous of all because they are usually much worse than true conditions. False gossip can ruin a reputation, and false rumors may start a riot.

I have no knowledge of all the rumors and accusations investigated, but I do know that when more than a hundred indictments were issued charging persons with crimes that were unknown when the jury began its hearings, there had to be a great amount of serious investigation.

The jury was highly critical of persons other than Chief Gustafsen, but not enough evidence could be found to prosecute. It was apparent that the county sheriff and the chief of the fire department should have been more alert.

The grand jury recognized that even the false rumors added to the tenseness of the situation. They helped to pile emotion on top of emotion until enough incidents were created to cause an explosion which led to the worst race riot in the history of this nation.

I realize that the last statement will be challenged by some, but facts cannot be denied. Some of the riots in recent years are better known because of so much news coverage, especially television, but by comparison, the total amount of damage done, and the number of deaths, the Tulsa riot makes most of the others seem but the play of children.

A town of approximately nine thousand people totally destroyed. With the exception of one schoolhouse (why it was left standing has always been a mystery, other schools were destroyed) all other buildings were burned to the ground. Not even a church or a house was left standing in the entire area. It seems unbelievable, but even the out-buildings where there was no indoor plumbing were destroyed.

At least one hundred persons were killed. Thirty white, and seventy Negros, and as explained earlier, maybe many more Negros were killed and cremated in the burning buildings. Also at least four hundred people wounded. This was death and destruction unmatched in the history of this nation. Not even a phenomenon of nature has been so destructive in this country.

This writer has several dozen clippings from newspapers and magazines relating the details of such riots as Detroit, Cleveland, Miami, Nashville, Newark, the Watts district etc., and in none of them was there anything near the horrible finale to the Tulsa riot. By today's standards, the property damage in Tulsa would be around eight or nine million dollars.

The only riot that even came close to matching the Tulsa horror, was the one years ago in East St. Louis, Illinois. It was very bad in property loss, area covered, and number of deaths. This is not a contest to decide which city is the champion in race rioting for there is not one thing that can be said on behalf of riots. All of them are terrible because innocent people are made homeless with everything that they own in the world being destroyed by man's hatred. Some are left suffering and dying from their wounds while others must grieve and mourn for their dead.

Since the purpose of this factual narration is to make known the horrible consequences that develop when people are foolish enough to agitate rioting conditions, the worst possible results must be told. The Tulsa riot is cited as an example because it typifies how suddenly race relations can change from at least a passive coexistence, into a raging rampage of killing and destruction by foolish agitation. The Tulsa riot is distinctive in other ways too; in the much larger size of the area destroyed, greater property loss, more dead and wounded, and the total displacement of the population of a city.

The entire population had either fled ahead of the mob, been killed, or wounded, or were interred in the jails, Convention Hall, or baseball park. Many of those that escaped across the hills, prairies, or river bottoms never returned to Tulsa. With all of their worldly goods destroyed and knowing that they would have to start over, many decided to do it in some other place. In no other city has an entire community been turned into rubble and ashes with not one Negro left alive in the entire area.

Also, in no other city has the majority race become involved in rioting by thousands on top of thousands. If a majority riots, no power is left to stop the destruction. Once started, the combined city and county enforcement agencies are not large enough to halt a raging mob. And before army units can be assembled and deployed, the killing and destroying rioters have had their day and everything is over but the bell tolling, and the weeping of the survivors.

In other cities, it was mentioned the rioting was by a small militant segment of a minority race. The majority of their own race did not join the extremists in burning and destroying. Therefore, the rioting was done by a small group who were not risking much because they had nothing to risk. Most professional agitators and their stooges are not property owners, so, they are not risking their own belongings when they agitate trouble.

Actually, Watts, Newark, Cleveland, Detroit, *et cetera*, were not race riots *per se*. A militant small fraction of the minority race rioted and destroyed some property then fought with the police authorities when they attempted to stop the destruction. Usually, the killings were limited to a militant or two, and a couple of police officers.

The white majority race and most of the Negros simply waited for the constituted authorities to bring the rioting under control. In each of the named places the actual number of persons involved, remained rather small. Consequently, the property damage was fairly high, but the dead and wounded count was low.

The lesson we must remember, is that when trouble is agitated to an explosion, its scope can't be limited. It can erupt into a Tulsa type holocaust where the damage is total destruction with hundreds wounded and killed. Playing with matches anytime is very dangerous, but when they are dropped into a powder-keg, even those who are agitating can be killed.

When agitators touched off the explosion in Tulsa no one dreamed that fifteen or eighteen thousand people would go on a rampage and destroy everything in their path leaving only a wasteland behind. Like a giant octopus with its tentacles reaching out in every direction, the mob swept through the Negro section of the city destroying, wounding, and killing as it went. It never stopped until it had reached and destroyed single houses here and there out in the fields and prairies beyond the city limits.

Not even a small house way out in the country, where someone had lived in order to have a little garden and orchard, was safe from the destroyers. The way some of the people rushed toward each little home made it seem that house destruction was all important, a sort of personal vendetta.

From the moment the large mob broke from behind the barricades of boxcars, buildings, and oilwell pipe, it seemed "Hellbent" on destroying everything down to the bare ground. Nothing could stop, or even slow it up until it had run its course. When there was nothing left to vent its anger upon, and from complete physical exhaustion, the mob simply faded away.

This is the real difference between a race riot, and a group of militants throwing a few bottles and bricks at a handful of police officers who are trying to prevent the destruction of a couple of buildings. Setting a few fires, throwing bottles, or even killing a police officer or two is not a race riot. A hundred or two malcontents bent on committing arson and wrecking some property while a few of their numbers snipe at some innocent people, wouldn't last as long as a snowball in the proverbial hot place. In a real riot, they would be crushed like a grape in a winepress.

Afterword

This writer began this report with multi-purpose intentions. First, to relate the terrible results, and the consequences of agitating race riots; to report in detail the horrible acts that are committed during periods of complete lawlessness when every man makes his own rules and hatred controls the actions of many persons; also, to describe the actual happenings as they occurred, and make this the most complete report of a race riot ever made.

I hope I have succeeded in the above. At the same time, I have been as objective as possible. Neither side has been reported as being worse than they actually were during the riot. In fairness, both sides must share the blame for the Tulsa race riot and the awful damage that occurred. The Negros because they committed the first foolish acts that started the riot. And the white people because they carried retaliation to unbelievable extremes.

Much of the early history of Tulsa has been related in this report so the reader may better understand the sort of people involved in the rioting.

Rumors, and the part they played in creating the conditions which exploded into a riot are narrated for the purpose of judging their harmfulness.

The actual incidents of killing, burning, and destroying during the riot points to the horrible consequences that occur when the hatred of people for those of other races runs rampant. This also exemplifies conditions of anarchy that occur when police authority fails to restrain those who are lawless.

The many organizations that assisted in the rebuilding by furnishing equipment, labor, materials, and money, proves that most people are the responsible sort that will always rise to the occasion during an emergency.

The speed with which the grand jury investigated, issued subpoenas and indictments for those inciting the riot, rioting, committing grand larceny, and other crimes is included in this report because the responsible members of Tulsa's population wished to show that they were not white-washing, or glossing over the stupid actions of the lawless element of its constituency.

Every word of this narration is true to the best of my memory, and the information gathered from other sources is exact as far as I can determine.

It is a multiple report consisting of the narration of an eyewitness who was present during the entire rioting period, statements of persons who were interviewed after answering advertisements in the newspapers, and days and days of researching every possible location for information, it can be said to be a complete report of a race riot from A to Z. Or a true profile of a race riot.

One of the first persons to answer the advertisement seeking information about the riot was Mr. Donald C. Hogan, an electrical contractor. During the interview he showed photographs taken during the riot. They came to Mr. Hogan in the personal effects of his late grandfather and were loaned to me for the purpose of having copies made.

Another group of snapshots was borrowed from Mrs. Verna M. Ward, who owns and operates a business in Tulsa. Many of the pictures of various scenes of the rioting were not usable for reprints because they were badly faded. Many photos are gruesome, but the actual scenes were worse.

Most of the persons interviewed were either reluctant to permit the use of their names as a source of information used in the manuscript, or they simply refused to allow the mentioning of their names in any manner. Nevertheless, I gratefully acknowledge the assistance of each of them and especially that of Donald C. Hogan and Mrs. Verna M. Ward.

Since the Massacre

Following the 1921 Tulsa Race Massacre, the grand jury assembled to investigate the incident returned approximately seventy indictments. Most of those were later dismissed. The grand jury report blamed the African Americans for inciting the riot. From there, the incident was pretty much swept under the rug of history and rarely discussed.

In 2001 an official Race Riot Commission was formed. Despite the number of years that had passed, several observations were made. First, the African Americans in Tulsa had every reason to believe Dick Rowland would be lynched following his arrest for assaulting a white girl due to the racial history and tensions of the time.

Local officials selected several white men when it appeared violence was imminent, even giving them weapons and ammunition. Not only did these men not stop the violence, they openly participated in the torching and killing that followed. Even when the Oklahoma National Guard was called in to quell the violence, it was too little too late, and they rounded up and interred the African American population.

The Riot Commission estimated that more than 1,250 homes were deliberately burned or otherwise destroyed. The mobs leveled approximately thirty-five square blocks of the city. The commission also determined that roughly 6,000 African Americans were detained, and an estimated 10,000 lost their homes. A final death toll has never been accurately determined but is estimated to be between 100 to more than 300. The City of Tulsa launched a search for mass graves in 2020 that was ongoing when this book was published.

In 2015 the Tulsa Race Riot Centennial Commission was announced with the objective being to educate pe0ple about the 1921 Tulsa Race Riot and the impact it had on Oklahoma and the nation. In addition, remember the victim and survivors, while fostering an environment that would promote sustainable entrepreneurship and heritage tourism within the Greenwood District and North Tulsa.

In 2018 Oklahoma officials announced a new curriculum that would help make sure Oklahoma students were made aware of and taught one of the nation's most violent racial events.

On August 4, 2021, Greenwood Rising opened in Tulsa and is dedicated to educating the public about the 1921 Tulsa Race Massacre. More than $30 million was raised by the Tulsa community to develop a state-of-the-art museum that utilizes history, technology, and interactive exhibits to provide a foundation to learn and discuss racial issues and the heritage of historically Black North Tulsa and the Greenwood District.

August 2, 2021

To Whom It May Concern:

My name is Stephanie Maggio and the following is my true accounting of what happened the summer of 1988.

William "Choc" Phillips was my grandfather. I called him Paw Paw, and to me, he was wonderful! He was a very reserved man who enjoyed watching from a distance the family gatherings on the farm in Leonard, Oklahoma. I believe he loved being able to provide the environment that we all got to enjoy. This is the grandfather I grew up with. He wouldn't say much, but always made sure I knew he loved me.

When Paw Paw asked me to come visit the summer of 1988, I was unsure why. I was 14 years old and had just finished my freshman year in high school. My mom had arranged for me to bring our new computer and dot matrix printer. When I arrived to the farm, he told me he wanted to tell me his eye witness account of what happened in 1921 in Tulsa, Oklahoma. This began my learning about the horrors of the 1921 race riots. He asked me to type as he talked. He was 87 years old, so he didn't talk for long periods of time, so when he would need to rest, I would type parts of the story that he had hand written or copy from papers he had typed over the years on his typewriter.

As he was recanting his story, there were numerous times when he became very emotional. A hugely impactful part for me was learning that in 1921, my Paw Paw was only a few years older than I was at the time I was typing. Just imagining the horror that he saw and hearing the story of the people who died horrible deaths, because of what...a girl who lied.

Our world changed that day in 1921, and for my grandfather, his life changed too. The lessons he learned made him want to become a police officer. Eventually, he did just that with the Tulsa Police Department and he changed many lives for the better in the process.

My grandfather, my Paw Paw, was a hero to me. A man not afraid to tell the truth about a horrible day in 1921.

Stephanie Maggio
Stephanie Maggio

State of _North Carolina_
County of _New Hanover_

I, _David Walters_ , a Notary Public, do hereby certify that on this _2_ day of
August , 2021, personally appeared before me _Stephanie Maggio_ ,
known to me to be the person whose name is subscribed to the foregoing instrument, and swore and acknowledged to me that she executed the same for the purpose and in the capacity therein expressed, and that the statements contained therein are true and correct.

Notary Public, State of _North Carolina_

Name, Typed or Printed: _David Walters_

My Commission Expires: _Dec 4, 2024_

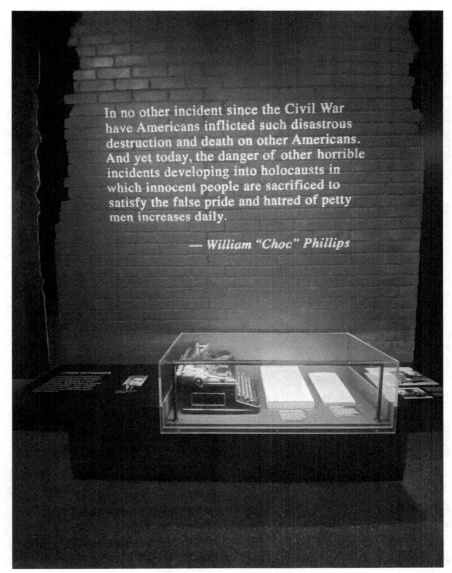

Today the original manuscript for this book and the typewriter used to produce it are part of the Greenwood Rising exhibits.

Greenwood Rising
23 N Greenwood Ave. • Tulsa, OK 74120
www.GreenwoodRising.org

Author Bio

William C. "Choc" Phillips was born Dec. 1, 1901, in Greer County, Okla., and moved with his family to Tulsa in 1918. His

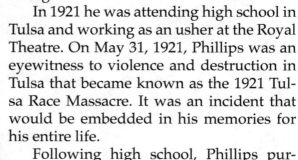

lineage?

In 1921 he was attending high school in Tulsa and working as an usher at the Royal Theatre. On May 31, 1921, Phillips was an eyewitness to violence and destruction in Tulsa that became known as the 1921 Tulsa Race Massacre. It was an incident that would be embedded in his memories for his entire life.

Following high school, Phillips pursued a career in show business as a vaudeville performer and show manager. In 1938 he was a founding member of the Society for the Preservation and Encouragement of Barber Shop Quartet Singing in America (SPEBSQSA), which would later be known as the Barbershop Quartet Society. Phillips also joined the Tulsa Police Department in 1938 as a member of their barbershop singing quartet that toured the United States promoting Tulsa.

During World War II, Phillips served in the U.S. Coast Guard before returning to his duties with Tulsa Police Department. During his police career, he was the president of the Fraternal Order of Police, formed the School Crossing Guard Program for the Tulsa public school system, and helped develop the Tulsa Police Retirement program that became a model for departments nationwide.

After retiring from the Tulsa Police Department, he became a cattle rancher in Leonard, Okla. In 1988 Phillips decided to put his memories and research of the 1921 Tulsa Race Massacre on paper and called on his niece, Stephanie Maggio, to assist him with the project. He continued ranching until his death on Dec. 10, 1991.

He was married to Annalee Elaine, his sweetheart whom he met while singing with his barbershop quartet group and the Tulsa Sweet Adelines, of which Elaine was a member. They had two children, Larry and Susan.

Index

11, 15
Univerity of Oklahoma 5
University of Tulsa 5, 122
University of Tulsa College of Law 5

W

Ward, Verna M. 136
Washington, Booker T. 3, 93
Washington D.C. 122
Watts, Calif. 132-133
Weathermen 123
White, Walter F. 119-121
World War I 19, 22, 54
World War II 1

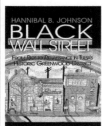
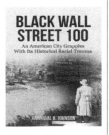

Printed in the USA
CPSIA information can be obtained
at www.ICGtesting.com
LVHW020915011123
762407LV00005B/17